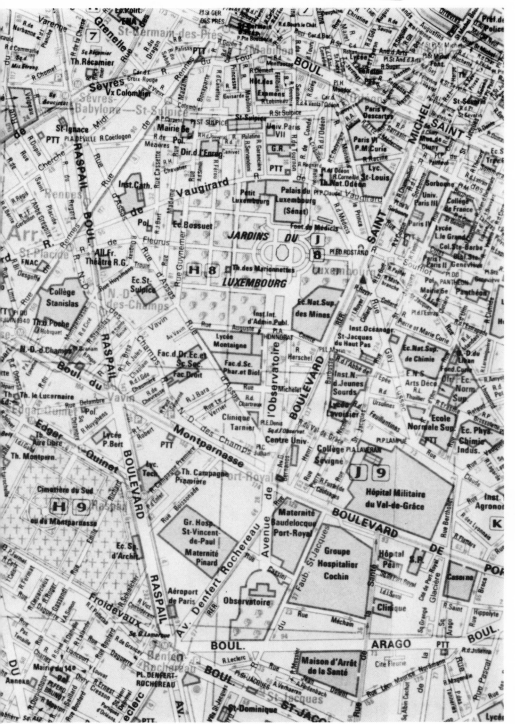

Map of Paris, the modern Left Bank area, courtesy of PCV Editions.

ON·THE LEFT·BANK 1929-1933

Wambly Bald

WAMBLY BALD

ON·THE
LEFT·BANK
1929-1933

·

EDITED BY

BENJAMIN FRANKLIN V

OHIO UNIVERSITY PRESS

ATHENS, OHIO LONDON

Introduction and notes © copyright 1987 by Benjamin Franklin V.
Printed in the United States of America.

Library of Congress Cataloging-in-Publication Data

Bald, Wambly.
  On the Left Bank, 1929-1933.

  Bibliography: p.
  Includes index.
  1. Paris (France)—Intellectual life—20th century.   2. Left Bank (Paris, France)—Intellectual life.   3. Americans—France—Paris—Biography. 4. Bohemianism—France—Paris—History—20th century.   I. Franklin, Benjamin, 1939-   . II. Title.
DC715.B22   1987   944'.3610815   86-23638
ISBN 0-8214-0852-6

to the memory of Benjamin Franklin IV

Unlike Caesar I came, I saw, but I didn't want to conquer. Being immersed in the soothing ambience of the world's slightly cockeyed cultural center in a Paris neighborhood known as Montparnasse was adequate purpose for me. I hope readers will get the message if there is one.

—WAMBLY BALD
December 1985

CONTENTS

INTRODUCTION

Americans writing in Paris during the 1920s formed the group that, with the exception of the great authors of the American Renaissance, created the most lasting work in America's literary history. Hemingway, Fitzgerald, and a few others will always be read, because of the fertility of their imaginations, their prose styles, and their pictures of the most romantic of literary eras. Paris in the twenties, before the stock market crash—with a few American dollars and few expenses, with numerous young authors struggling to find their literary voices and develop their craft, with an atmosphere of liberality and understanding and a dedication to artistic expression—was the best of times. But such conditions could not last, and they did not. The stock market soared and sank; financial realities set in. The young, bright writers returned to the country that they had written about in Paris. But while Hemingway and others left Paris, some Americans, many of them women, remained. Gertrude Stein continued to hold forth at the art-bedecked apartment she shared with Alice B. Toklas. Djuna Barnes stayed in Paris, as did the publishers Sylvia Beach and Caresse Crosby. Other Americans arrived, most notably Henry Miller, then unpublished, unknown, and impoverished. And of course non-American artists who had created and would create some of this century's most important work also lived there. Need I mention Picasso, Joyce, and Stravinsky? In other words, Paris is, for artists, a permanent as well as a moveable feast.

Paris of the 1920s is one of the most chronicled of literary eras, and for good reason. Considerably less well known is artistic Paris of the next decade. As the 1930s progressed, grave concern over the worldwide economic depression was replaced in Europeans' minds by Hitler's threat. Serious practical concerns threatened everybody. Nonetheless, severe social and political conditions did not keep the likes of Fernand Léger and others from seeking the new in art. Avant-garde Paris knew about them, as did interested Americans who read Janet Flanner's long-running column "Letter from Paris" in the *New Yorker*. She reported the activities and accomplishments of these artists as well as those of such figures as Jean Cocteau and Stein. (She also profiled Hitler.) Flanner, writing as Genêt, is one of the best sources of information about artists active in Paris in the 1930s. Among others who have written about them in memoirs are Samuel Putnam, Beach, and Crosby. Such recent scholars as Hugh Ford and George Wickes have analyzed them from a critical perspective; a volume of the *Dictionary of Literary Biography* is devoted to them and to the writers of the 1920s.[1]

Paris is usually thought of in two parts: the Right Bank and the Left Bank. The former, north of the Seine, is what the tourists see, or at least the wealthy ones or the ones on expense accounts. It has the fashionable shops, the Louvre, the Opéra, and the Arc de Triomphe. It is *au courant*. The Left Bank, on the other side of the river, is, traditionally, just the opposite, although less so now than formerly. Specifically, in the area known as Montparnasse, Bohemianism reigns. The aberrant is normal; art—and especially the avant-garde—is its lifeblood. It is alive. Into this colorful scene, just before the stock market crash, came Wambly Bald, who was then unknown to anyone in Paris. Born on 12 February 1902 in Chicago, where he grew up, he attended Tuley High School, from which he was graduated in 1918, and the University of Chicago, from which he took a bachelor of philosophy degree in 1924. During his college years he frequented the Dill Pickel Club, on the near north side, an area which was then Chicago's version of Greenwich Village. His experiences there foreshadowed his life in Montparnasse and prepared him for it. With college behind him, he wished to teach philosophy and psychology; instead, for reasons unknown he took jobs selling first chocolate and then Blatz beer to retailers. Then, following the philosophy of Whitman and Jack London, he became a self-professed "bum," an existence he loved. He took to the road and the rails. Pride kept him from hitchhiking, and he rarely took freight trains. Instead, he rode the blinds, risking injury if not his life by pulling himself aboard moving passenger trains. He traveled west to work in the fields harvesting grain. Then, serving as an ordinary seaman with New Orleans as his home port, he sailed for Europe in 1929. Although he planned to stay there for only a few weeks, he became attracted to the cultural life in Paris generally and Montparnasse specifically, and he decided to stay.

Being enamored of Montparnasse is one thing; living there is another. One needs money to survive, and Bald, unemployed, had little of it. At the zinc bar of the Dôme café, he learned that a proofreader for the European edition of the *Chicago Tribune* had, because of a death in the family, returned to the United States. In time, Bald drifted to the paper, where he was hired to fill the vacant position. Among his fellow proofreaders were Henry

Miller and Alfred Perlès. Once Jules Frantz, the managing editor, got to know Bald, he correctly perceived the newcomer as a hobo with a college degree, as a romantic, as a philosophic vagabond who would likely fit in with the free spirits of Montparnasse. As a result, Frantz asked the inexperienced Bald to write about the characters of Montparnasse in a new weekly column, "La Vie de Bohème."

It became an immediate hit with the cognoscenti, with the café habitués, with those interested in gossip about artists of all kinds. It became such a fixture that readers eagerly awaited the publication of each new column to see whether they or their friends would be mentioned in it. If they were, they gritted their teeth and read it. (Bald does not always position his subjects in the best light.) If not, they read it anyway. They found it magnetic.

Bald's column occasionally treats members of the literary establishment, such as Sinclair Lewis, as they pass through Paris; but most often it features the less exalted, the regulars of Montparnasse, the people who created and promoted the new, which did not always become the lasting, as history has shown. Is Virginia Hersch read today? Or Eric Walrond? Or Aleister Crowley, for that matter? Most people now know of Louise Bryant, if at all, as John Reed's wife in the movie *Reds*, and not as Bald's Bryant—the author of books about the Soviet Union, the aviatrix, or the woman who had a room next to a nunnery. The most serious artists, the ones whose creations have endured, were great in part because they pursued their art and craft and did not dally with the Bohemians. Lasting art does not result from posturing.

That many of Bald's subjects are largely forgotten does not matter. Bald's territory was Montparnasse, a world, as Francis Dickie has written, "where the genius, the commonplace, the eccentric, and the mad move upon fantastically twisted paths."[2] Bald charts these paths and encounters the genius (May Ray), the commonplace (Rosalie), the eccentric (Kiki), and the mad (Henri Broca). Bald knew and wrote about the personalities who congregated in or visited Montparnasse. For this reason, his column is valuable, and doubtless more so now than then. He describes, as no one else has done, Mergault and Petroff, Gwen Le Gallienne, Contessa Lina Monici, and Dolores (or Doris) Carlyle. He offers a new perspective on Raymond Duncan, Link Gillespie, and Countee Cullen. He gives Henry Miller his first publicity. Ultimately, he became known, correctly, as "the Left Bank's ubiquitous Boswell."[3]

Because Bald creates a picture, a mood, a sense of personality and time and place, he is not overly concerned with factual accuracy, although often he obviously researches his topic and provides facts, such as information about Maryse Choisy, that are difficult to find elsewhere. But while the fame of his subjects is of no consequence, neither is his refusal to let facts stand in the way of a good story. For example, in his fullest treatment of Gertrude Stein, in his column of 7 April 1931, he reports her as saying that her *The Making of Americans* was published in 1905 and therefore antedated Joyce's *Ulysses* by seventeen years. Even if one knows that Stein's book was published in 1925, three years after *Ulysses*, Bald's magnificent portrait of "she who looks like Caesar" does not suffer. This column above all others illustrates that personality and not fact lends "La Vie de Bohème" its charm.

If occasional inaccurate factual information is a nonproblem in "La Vie de Bohème," so too is the issue of authorship. Some published evidence suggests that Henry Miller at least helped his friend Bald write some of the columns. In a letter to Anaïs Nin from Dijon, dated 13 February 1932, Miller relates that he and Bald once interviewed Djuna Barnes. He does not imply that he helped Bald write about Barnes, but he does suggest that he accompanied Bald at least once on field work, since Bald wrote about Barnes (most significantly in his column of 2 September 1931). But two months later, in April 1932, from Clichy, Miller again writes to Nin, explaining that he had recently made a breakfast appointment with Bald to "help him write his column." He quotes Bald as saying, "We gotta write a good column." Then, in a scene that seems improbable, at best, Miller tells that he wrote the column as he drank a bottle of Cointreau while Bald, in the same room, was having sexual intercourse with a woman. And finally, in a letter to Nin from Clichy in March 1933, Miller mentions Bald's use of the word *ygdrasil* in a column and states that he, Miller, "had nothing to do with it." The antecedent of *it* is vague. Does he mean the column or the word? If he means the column, he might imply that he had helped Bald with earlier columns. (The column to which Miller refers is that of 28 February 1933.) Then, in Miller's *Tropic of Cancer* (1934), the narrator tells of having to write a column for Van Norden, a character obviously based on Bald. Since fiction does not equal fact, even in Miller's autobiographical novels, this statement constitutes no evidence at all. Next, Alfred Perlès, who appears as Carl in *Tropic of Cancer*, published, in 1955, a book about his long-time friend Miller. In it, he notes that because Bald has difficulty submitting his copy on time, Bald occasionally turns to Perlès and Miller for assistance. As a quid pro quo, Bald brings an occasional meal to the desperately hungry Miller.[4]

To this day Bald insists that he alone wrote his column. The truth will probably never be known, although the published evidence does not prove that Miller—or Perlès—helped him write it. Jules Frantz has written, "I, for one, don't buy Perlès's story that Miller sometimes wrote Bald's column for him."[5] Frantz, the man who, as editor, read Bald's copy, is probably the most reliable source on this issue. The fact that the primary document, the column itself, is consistent throughout in style and tone and personality, thus suggests that one person wrote it all. Of course others doubtless gave Bald ideas and information and accompanied him on interviews, but such assistance does not constitute authorship. Every column after the first bears Bald's name as author; he likely wrote all one hundred ninety-four columns.[6]

One of the charms of "La Vie de Bohème" is Bald's own voice. He has opinions, which are usually irreverent, and a point of view. These, and a genial personality, make him eminently likeable. Art generally and literature specifically are areas about which he expresses his opinions freely. He calls Marcel Duchamp, for example, a "one-picture man" (column of 6 January 1931). Clearly Bald is wrong: Duchamp is important for more than *Nude Descending a Staircase,* but once again the fact—or opinion—is less significant than the spirit. Occasionally Bald provides genuine insight, as he does into Modigliani's frustrations. Most significantly, he chronicles the appearance of various little magazines, analyzes their contents, and criticizes their contributors. This is especially true with the *New Review,* which Samuel Putnam (Marlowe in *Tropic of Cancer*) edited from January 1931 to April 1932, first in Paris and then in Mirmande. In fact, Bald comments on it so regularly that Perlès claims that Bald was Putnam's "unpaid press agent."[7]

Press agent or not, but certainly unpaid for whatever publicity he provides, Bald comments frequently on the *New Review.* On 8 October 1930 he prepares his readers for the first number and announces that Montparnasse is already buzzing about it. Such concern in the cafés seems unlikely, but, given the context, perhaps the Left Bank was interested in Putnam's publication, which would not be published for three months. Putnam, who in 1930 had helped Edward W. Titus edit the periodical *This Quarter,* disagreed with Titus over the merit of James T. Farrell's fiction. Putnam liked it; Titus did not. One thing led to another, and Putnam began thinking seriously about literary theory. He concluded that Eugene Jolas's *transition,* the major little magazine of the day and possibly of all time, encourages form at the expense of content, which struck Putnam as wrong. To combat this attitude, Putnam, Harold Salemson, and Richard Thoma published their literary philosophy in "Direction," a placard that they distributed to the Montparnasse cafés in late October 1930. Putnam then established the *New Review* to promulgate his theories, to publish writers who shared his ideas, and to do friendly battle with Jolas and *transition*.[8] Bald is therefore probably correct in maintaining that the *New Review* was the object of much discussion well before it was published.

In addition to anticipating the publication of the various numbers of the *New Review*, Bald devotes his entire column of 27 January 1931 to discussing the first number, which, with the exception of an essay by Maxwell Bodenheim, he likes. Most of his 14 April 1931 column focuses on the second number, about which he also has reservations. He details the third number in his column of 19 August 1931; he loves the fiction and detests the essays. But by the time Putnam took the *New Review* with him from Paris to Mirmande following the publication of the third number, Bald had apparently grown weary of it. He ignores the fourth number, and he excoriates the fifth, which was also the last.

The columns do not support Perlès's contention that Bald was the *New Review*'s press agent or that, by extension, he was Putnam's toady. Yes, he publicizes four of the five numbers, but he is often critical of the magazine's contents. And when Bald addresses the *New Review* and *transition* in the same column (22 March 1932), he praises both editors, Putnam and Jolas, and both publications. Bald's column is one of the best contemporary commentaries on the Parisian little magazines of the early 1930s: the *New Review, transition*, and even *This Quarter*.

One reason for his extensive treatment of the *New Review* might be that Bald himself appears in the first three numbers, not as a columnist, but as a fiction writer and as an essayist/reviewer. Never in his column does he mention this fact. Actually, the two short stories are his first efforts at fiction and constitute two-thirds of his fictional output.

Bald's fiction, which is generally surrealistic, gloomy, and a bit absurd, does not appear to be more concerned with content than form. If anything, his technique is dazzling and his message is vague. "From Work in Static," his first published story, if such it may be called, appears in the initial number of the *New Review*. It is in two distinct, unrelated parts, "(Extract from 'The Woman with the Broken Nose')" and "The Dells of Dahlia." Each is a brief dramatic dialogue: in the first part between a man and a woman; in the second, among a man, a woman, a ferry conductor, and, briefly, the passengers on the boat. Each part begins with a description of the scene.

The first part is set in a wasteland at night. Into it walks a frightened man, an artist, wearing torn pajamas; toward him rushes a woman who believes that they are in hell. She, the more sensible of the two, the one more attuned to reality, attempts to understand the man, but she cannot. He speaks in riddles:

> Woman: Why do you paint?
> Man: To keep myself in pyjamas.
> Woman: Express yourself simply. I'm only a woman.
> Man: If I didn't paint, I would be naked, depyjamaed. I would be anonymous. People would ignore my existence. I would be lonesome. It's very simple.
> Woman: But your pyjamas are in a terrible condition.
> Man: Yes. I was beginning to lose faith and so I started to tear them off. (Sobs).
> Woman: Don't cry. I like you without your pyjamas.
> Man: (cynically) You think so. Without these ragged pyjamas, I would have only a bare body. No significance to society—no comprehensible self. Every man needs a label, a meaning, a pair of pyjamas. Men paint and write because they want to love themselves and they can't love themselves until the world loves them and the world will not love them until they manage to wear a nice pair of pyjamas. No man ever paints or writes for any other reason, but the average artist ass doesn't know it. Are you following me?[9]

The woman's nose is likely out of joint, if not broken.

The second part concerns a ferry trip to the dells of Dahlia, possibly the underworld, where Mimi, the Charon-like ferry conductor, satisfies the passengers' sexual desires. Before the boat sails, a man named John and an unnamed woman prepare to board. They perceive the situation accurately and, at the woman's insistence, decide not to accompany Mimi and the others. Bald's point seems to be that while the majority succumb to Mimi's charms, a few are able to resist temptation. These few do not appear to be morally superior to the others on the ferry, since Mimi's last words are for John to contact her again tomorrow, when, without the company of his woman friend, he will possibly board Mimi's bark. Bald might mean that such an action—going with Mimi—is desirable.

Bald's second piece in the *New Review*, "New Garters for Apollo," is an abstruse essay that focuses on two anonymous books, *Werther's Younger Brother* (written by Michael Fraenkel) and *USA with Music* (by Walter Lowenfels), in order to denounce the rise of various artistic movements.[10] Fraenkel and Lowenfels were friends of Henry Miller's, and both books, about death, were published by their own Carrefour Press. The most memorable part of Bald's essay is its title.

If "New Garters for Apollo" is of little consequence, Bald's next and last contribution to the *New Review*, "Dreary," is his most sustained and best piece of fiction. Set in Paris and told from the decadent Ian's point of view, the story concerns her lesbian relationship with Taffy. Bald maintains suspense as he portrays men and women high on dope and with their libidos unencumbered.

At the outset, the world-weary Ian awakens at 3:00 P.M., with her lover beside her. The reader knows that Ian is a woman, but Bald withholds Taffy's name and gender until the two women are well along in their love making, which lasts for five hours. Ian—she with a man's name—loves cheap affairs. She also likes to catch flies and squeeze them to death. In her dreariness, she never quite faces reality.

Ian and Taffy's affair does not go smoothly, as Taffy, who is notoriously unfaithful, entertains both men (Stanley) and women (Kate), to Ian's disgust. When Taffy finally leaves her, Ian walks the streets alone looking for companionship. At the Tangerine Club she meets Mrs. Firming, a large American whose husband has recently left her. After dancing together, Ian and Mrs. Firming have the following exchange:

> "You are a stupid person, Mrs. Firming."
> "I've been told about your type. You're the kind that likes women. I knew it the minute I laid eyes on you," said the woman.
> Ian's eyes were hot and steady. They were watching Mrs. Firming. They stared right in. Mrs. Firming tried to smile.
> Ian said: "You are a *very* vulgar person and somehow you look like a crocodile. Especially when you drink beer. You look very animal when you drink beer. And I hate the way you grin. Stop grinning—for Christ's sake."[11]

To illustrate these women's desperation for human connection, this odd couple—neither can abide the other—goes to Ian's apartment for an evening of love making.

Despite Ian's hard exterior, she is vulnerable. She might think that she prefers cheap affairs to substantial ones, but she does not. She is unhappy, depressed. As a result, she shoots herself to death on a park bench.

Bald titled this story perfectly. Ian is dreary, but so is everyone else: Taffy, Mrs. Firming, Kate, Jock, Harold, Helen, the Count, Eustace, Vic, a sailor, and possibly Stanley. They use heroin, cocaine, and opium. Most of the men are homosexual; the women, lesbian. But as with "From Work in Static," Bald is not being moralistic; he is not pointing the finger. He is, as in his *Tribune* column, creating a mood and capturing personality that is outside the bourgeois experience. In his column, he depicts the Bohemians; in his fiction, the seamy side of life.

Readies for Bob Brown's Machine, in which Bald's "Flow Gently" appears, is dated 1931, but it was not published until January 1932. "Flow Gently" is Bald's last published story. Bob Brown, with Ross Saunders's and possibly Hilaire Hiler's assistance, created a machine to help speed the reading process and save space. A reader views the text, in small type on tape, through a magnifying glass as the tape passes through the machine. It is similar in concept to reading microfilm. Such authors as Laurence Vail, Nancy Cunard, Link Gillespie, and Bald wrote specifically for this project, and they write, expectedly, in an unorthodox manner. They use odd punctuation and capitalization, for example. Little is stylistically predictable. (See Bald's columns of 19 May 1931 and 19 January 1932.) "Flow Gently" incorporates these unusual devices and adds a strong element of onomatopoeia. The story is set in a train car. The first words, "Dark a de rain a de cold a de bang a de bang the train like hell," create the sound of the train's wheels on the track.[12] But the rhythm thus established does not reflect the events of the story. After boarding a baggage car in Baton Rouge, Lefty is diverted from his suffering in the cold night air by someone else in the car. Surprisingly, it is a seventeen-year-old named Joan, dressed as a man. When he attempts to rape her, she shoves him through the doorway and into the water that flows gently beneath the bridge.

Once again Bald creates characters who live on the fringe of society. Like Bald himself as a young man, Lefty rides the rails, but he is not a philosophic vagabond, as his creator was. He is a desperate, frustrated man who dies after attempting to force himself on another. In this and his other two stories, Bald focuses on the outsiders, the pariahs, not to illustrate that such characters are malcontents or misfits—although they are—but rather to depict the level to which some people plummet and the grief that they are forced to endure. Two of his protagonists—Ian and Lefty—die. In a sense, he is a naturalist in the tradition of someone like Theodore Dreiser. But since he wrote only three short stories, too much should not be made of them. They serve best to show that Bald could write well in an idiom other than journalism and that, because of where the stories were published, he was regarded as a substantial writer by the avant-garde of the day. He showed enough promise, though, for Richard Thoma to consider him "the greatest living non-writer."[13]

Bald is obviously most important not as a fiction writer but as the author of "La Vie de Bohème," and so he was viewed in the early 1930s. In fact, his column became so popular that Erskine Gwynne, editor of the *Boulevardier*, a slick monthly reminiscent of the *New Yorker*, asked Bald to write a column for that Right Bank publication. He did. From September 1931 through January 1932 (and possibly through February 1932; no copy of this number—the *Boulevardier*'s last—is known to exist), Bald wrote "The Left-Over Bank," a column that for some time had been a regular feature in the magazine. The column is similar, in its irreverent voice, to "La Vie de Bohème." In it he comments on O. O. McIntyre, Samuel Putnam, Djuna Barnes, Jimmie, Kiki, Dolores Carlyle, Gwen Le Gallienne, J. P. McEvoy, Man Ray, Adolf Dehn, and others who appear in his *Tribune* column. Bald obviously did not take this new assignment seriously: he fails to develop character or mood. The following, the last paragraph of the January 1932 column, illustrates Bald's technique in the *Boulevardier*:

> A few good citizens have left. Charley Gorman, one of the Joyce biographers, went to New York to negotiate another book in that line. Frances Gest, a charming hostess who comes here now and then, will give her next parties in Nice. And while Alexander Altenburg returned to his villa in Cagnes, the sociable Kathleen O'Connor was taken to Monte Carlo in a Hispano-Suiza. Richard Le Gallienne is returning to Menton for the next few cold months, and Mary Coles is on her way to Majorca where she won't be bothered. Mable Rite's [sic] Venetian boy friend hasn't come to her, so she's going to him. Probably to wreck his gondola, judging from her mood. Anne Ritchie says it's true, and she is going to have it done for nothing in Poland. But Ford Maddox Ford [sic], the grand old cavalier, has returned from Toulon.[14]

Occasionally in "La Vie de Bohème" he uses such information as filler, but his concern there, in his regular column, is broader, more ambitious, and eminently more readable and successful than in "The Left-Over Bank."

Bald's celebrity as a journalist—and specifically as a chronicler of Montparnasse—spread from the Left Bank to the Right, but it also spread to the United States. Since *Vanity Fair* wished to inform its readers about the current events in and the mood of the Left Bank, someone at the magazine asked him to write about it. His "Montparnasse Today" appears in the issue of July 1932. Here he debunks the popular myth of Montparnasse as a place of orgies and dedicated artists. The tourist expecting to find such uninhibited behavior and serious people will be disappointed, because the visitor really sees "a congested little colony with an Ellis Island atmosphere. Misfits of all nations crowd into the numerous cafés or flock at the tables placed very close together on the sidewalks."[15] In other words, the reality is more mundane than one expects it to be. Bald tells about jazz clubs and gigolos taking over Montparnasse and of luminaries leaving the Left Bank: Kay Boyle and Laurence Vail, Emma Goldman and Alexander Berkman, and Paul Morand and Michael Arlen, among others. He also addresses the Montparnasse literary issue of the day—form versus content—by reporting about the Joyce-influenced *transition* (exemplified by Link Gillespie) and Putnam's *New Review*, with its insistence on clarity. In the end, Bald avers that Montparnasse no longer exists geographically, that it "has become an idea."[16]

Perhaps what Bald perceived as the real Montparnasse ceased to exist by mid 1932. Certainly in "La Vie de Bohème" he charts the people who are leaving: the Countess, Harold Stearns, Link Gillespie, Adolf Dehn, and Rosalie. Nonetheless, almost forty years after his last *Tribune* column, Bald wrote again about the Left Bank. In January 1971 he did so for Hugh Ford's *The Left Bank Revisited*, a wonderful book that features numerous selections from the *Tribune*. Bald figures prominently in it, for which he wrote "The Sweet Madness of Montparnasse."[17] Gracefully written, this reminiscence succeeds in capturing the mood of the Left Bank in the early 1930s. Both generally and specifically it is similar to his *Vanity Fair* piece: he recreates the *c'est la vie* attitude of the time and comments on such acquaintances as Jimmie, Kiki, Colette, Man Ray, Paul Morand, James Stephens, Ezra Pound, Ford Madox Ford, Henry Miller, Alfred Perlès, and Hemingway.

But Bald had not finished writing about Montparnasse. In 1974 and again in 1983 he wrote about it for *Lost Generation Journal*. The earlier piece, "I Remember Miller," expands upon his account of Henry Miller in Ford's book. To Bald, Miller looked like Bert Lahr and sounded like Senator Everett Dirksen. In the second, "Ah Paris!" Bald reminisces about *poules*, American housewives and coeds visiting Paris to lose their inhibitions, cafés, Kiki, Pound, Augustus John, Hemingway, Dos Passos, and Bald himself.[18]

So writes Bald about the Left Bank, about Montparnasse of the late 1920s and early 1930s. No one else has written about it with such verve, such style, such vividness. His greatest accomplishment is clearly the picture he creates in "La Vie de Bohème," a picture that is filtered through his own engaging personality. How close to the mark Samuel Putnam is in his 1947 comment on Bald cannot now be determined, but it offers one friend's recollection of him as a reporter: he "was in the habit of wandering in and out of the Quarter like a slightly alcoholic ghost, seeing nothing, hearing nothing, and telling all."[19] We have seen that Bald is not always factually accurate, but we have also seen how facts are less important in this case than mood, personality, spirit of place. Sisley Huddleston recognized this. Within a week of Bald's last *Tribune* column, Huddleston writes about "La Vie de Bohème" in a letter to the *Tribune*'s editor. He praises the column and states that Bald's Montparnasse "is worthy . . . to be set beside Ruritania and Erewhon and Utopia and Atlantis and Laputa and all the other legendary kingdoms and republics which are far more living than, say, America."[20] And indeed it is.

Bald's career after Paris is as difficult to document as are his years before 1929. He likes to relate that Hemingway paid for his trip from Paris to the United States. Bald, who was, he believes, Hemingway's favorite columnist, met Hemingway in the Luxembourg Gardens. The following dialogue ensued:

Hemingway: Where is everybody?
Bald: They've all gone back to the States.
Hemingway: Don't you want to return?
Bald: I don't know.
Hemingway: If you do, I'll pay your way.
Bald: Why not?
Hemingway: Here's the money.[21]

So Bald returned to the United States, thanks, apparently, to Hemingway.

Bald soon began working for the *New York American* as editor of the "March of Events" section, and he stayed with the paper until late 1937, until after it became the *Journal-American*. Upon quitting the paper and moving to California, he read movie scripts for the studios. That assignment probably ended around the beginning of World War II, during which time Bald served as a news writer for the Office of War Information. He also freelanced as a writer of what he calls "true confessions" pieces. Shortly after the war ended he edited a publication for an industrial firm in Albany, New York; afterward he took what was, in all likelihood, his last real job: that as feature writer for the *New York Post* from 1951 to 1954. What Bald did for the next thirty years is unclear. At one point he traveled to Paris in an effort to reexperience the Montparnasse of the 1930s. Of course he could not: it had changed, as, doubtless, had he. Disillusioned, he returned to the United States for the last time. He worked for a while as a freelancer and has lived for many years in Greenwich Village.

Bald has outlived almost all of the people he wrote about. Kay Boyle and George Seldes are two who, at this writing, survive. Although an arthritic hip inhibits Bald's movement and a hearing problem makes speaking with him difficult, this lifelong bachelor has a vivid memory of Montparnasse. He is able—and quite willing—to relate the facts or impressions that might be inferred only from reading his column: Louise Bryant was a drunk, Bryant and Gwen Le Gallienne were lovers, Le Gallienne wore jockey shorts, Lillian Fisk looked like a dwarf, Ralph Cheever Dunning was an opium fiend, Contessa Lina Monici kidnapped Bald in hopes that he would write her memoirs (and she proved to him that she was a "real blonde"), Eugene Jolas was confused because he grew up speaking three languages, Alfred Perlès was pathetic, and so forth.

Bald's memories of life in Paris over half a century ago might be tantalizing, but readers of his column need no supplementary information in order to enjoy it. It stands on its own. And in the end, Bald himself is unimportant to the reader of his column, except as its author, as the voice that relates the events. In other words, the facts of his life have little if any bearing on what he wrote. The column reflects his spirit and personality as a young man in his late twenties and early thirties: he avoided the temptation or inclination to become, as many people that age do, serious about himself. He had no family responsibilities; he was a free spirit. He could leave work at the *Tribune* at 2:00 A.M. and carouse with Henry Miller at the Dôme. He could sleep until noon. And what better place was there to be thirty and carefree than Paris, and especially Montparnasse? The personalities were there to experience and write about—Gillespie, Stein, Jimmie, Flossie Martin, and the rest. All that was needed to bring their character to life was someone with a reporter's nose for a good story, someone who could write, someone slightly cynical, someone with a sardonic sense of humor. All that was needed, of course, was Wambly Bald.

Bald's text is reproduced courtesy of the Chicago Tribune Company. Lee Major, the *Tribune* archivist, performed extraordinary service. Jo, Abigail, and Rebecca Jane Franklin and Jane Taft helped me establish the text. George Geckle funded research in Chicago and New York. The Interlibrary Loan and Reference departments at the Thomas Cooper Library, University of South Carolina, solved many research problems, as did librarians at other institutions. Colleagues at the University of South Carolina and elsewhere graciously answered my questions and provided other valuable services. Donald Greiner, Kenneth Craven, Mura Dehn, Freeman Henry, Robert Tibbetts, and Matthew Bruccoli were especially helpful.

B.F.
March 1986

NOTES

1. See Janet Flanner, *Paris Was Yesterday 1925–1939*, ed. Irving Drutman (New York: Viking, 1972); Samuel Putnam, *Paris Was Our Mistress Memoirs of a Lost & Found Generation* (New York: Viking, 1947); Sylvia Beach, *Shakespeare and Company* (New York: Harcourt, Brace, 1959); Caresse Crosby, *The Passionate Years* (New York: Dial, 1953); *The Left Bank Revisited: Selections from the Paris "Tribune" 1917–1934*, ed. Hugh Ford (University Park and London: Pennsylvania State University Press, 1972); Ford, *Published in Paris American and British Writers, Printers, and Publishers in Paris, 1920–1939* (New York: Macmillan, 1975); George Wickes, *Americans in Paris* (Garden City: Doubleday/Paris Review Editions, 1969); *American Writers in Paris, 1920–1939*, ed. Karen Lane Rood (Detroit: Gale Research/Bruccoli Clark, 1980).
2. Francis Dickie, "Modern Montparnasse," *The World Today*, 58.2 (July 1931), pp. 105–14. The quotation is from p. 106.
3. Ford, *The Left Bank Revisited*, p. 91.
4. See Henry Miller, *Letters to Anaïs Nin*, ed. Gunther Stuhlmann (New York: Putnam's, 1965), pp. 32, 37–38, 89 (the quotations are from pp. 37, 38, 89); Miller, *Tropic of Cancer* (New York: Grove Press, 1961), p. 170; Alfred Perlès, *My Friend Henry Miller* (London: Neville Spearman, 1955), pp. 21–22.
5. Ralph Jules Frantz, "Recollections," in *The Left Bank Revisited*, pp. 308–16. The quotation is from p. 312.
6. Jay Martin claims that Miller "occasionally wrote part of the column himself, for ten francs" and that he wrote the column about himself (the column of 14 October 1931). See Martin, *Always Merry and Bright: The Life of Henry Miller* (Santa Barbara: Capra Press, 1978), pp. 210, 241. The quotation is from p. 210. Martin offers no evidence to support his statements.
7. Perlès, p. 32.
8. For a discussion of these events, see Putnam, pp. 108–9, 156, 226–28.
9. Wambly Bald, "From Work in Static," *New Review*, 1.1 (January-February 1931), pp. 55–57. The quotation is from p. 56.
10. Bald, "New Garters for Apollo," *New Review*, 1.2 (May-June-July 1931), pp. 146–48.
11. Bald, "Dreary," *New Review*, 1.3 (August-September-October 1931), pp. 50–58. The quotation is from p. 57. "Dreary" also appears in *Americans Abroad An Anthology*, ed. Peter Neagoe (The Hague: Servire, 1932), pp. 8–18.
12. Bald, "Flow Gently," *Readies for Bob Brown's Machine*, ed. Bob Brown (Cagnes-sur-Mer: Roving Eye Press, 1931), pp. 60–61. The quotation is from p. 60.
13. Richard Thoma, quoted in Tom Wood, "Bald Trapped in Miller's Fiction," *Lost Generation Journal*, 6.2 (Winter 1980), pp. 8–9. The quotation is from p. 9.

14. Bald, "The Left-Over Bank," *Boulevardier*, 6.1 (January 1932), pp. 26, 28. The quotation is from p. 28.
15. Bald, "Montparnasse Today," *Vanity Fair*, 38.5 (July 1932), pp. 31, 58. The quotation is from p. 31.
16. Bald, "Montparnasse Today," p. 58.
17. Bald, "The Sweet Madness of Montparnasse," in *The Left Bank Revisited*, pp. 284-89.
18. Bald, "I Remember Miller," *Lost Generation Journal*, 2.3 (Fall 1974), pp. 38-41; "Ah Paris!" *Lost Generation Journal*, 7.3 (Winter 1983), pp. 9-11.
19. Putnam, pp. 106-7.
20. Sisley Huddleston, letter to the editor, *Chicago Tribune* (European edition), 31 July 1933, p. 4.
21. Bald related this dialogue—and much of the biographical information in this introduction—to me at the Overseas Press Club, New York City, on 11 October 1985.

TEXTUAL NOTE

I have silently added or deleted the few commas necessary to make syntactical sense; never have I done so to satisfy my own stylistic preference. I have corrected Bald's occasionally incorrect spelling (Ford Maddox Ford, for example) and have made consistent his inconsistent spelling (Jimmy, Jimmie), capitalization (surrealism, Surrealism), and use of quotation marks, diacritical marks, and italics. I have placed within quotation marks the titles of book chapters, poems, and the like. I have bracketed the few words that syntax required that I add to the text, and I have inserted [*sic*] when I could not determine whether Bald intended a word to appear as it does. Occasionally in his text a colon precedes a short quotation that he makes into a new paragraph. I have reunited such sentences. In a few instances I have blocked off a long quotation. I have deleted beginning and ending quotation marks from block quotations and have changed such quotations from italic to roman type. I have corrected the ellipses. Triple asterisks indicate a paragraph or paragraphs deleted; a single asterisk signifies the conclusion of a column. With these exceptions, this text duplicates Bald's. "La Vie de Bohème" contains illustrations to which Bald occasionally refers. The originals are lost, and because the extant copies are brittle and the illustrations are not sharp, they cannot be reproduced. (The illustrations of Gwen Le Gallienne, Aleister Crowley, and Henri Broca, which appeared originally in the *Tribune*, are reproduced from Hugh Ford's *The Left Bank Revisited*.)

Monday, 21 October 1929, p. 4.

The face of the Left Bank wears a mask during the summer months. It is only with the advent of the autumn chill and the ensuing colder weather that the Quarter is revealed in all its mellow glory. They say the district hibernates not in winter, but in the summer time. Perhaps the impersonality of the crowded terraces, with their distracting sights and sounds, is responsible. But they are commencing to go inside now, where one doesn't have to shout and where cliques and groups may dream or talk without the sweetened Coney Island flavor.

Tihanyi is coming back to Montparnasse. Lajos Tihanyi, the Hungarian genius whose name is often mentioned in the same breath with that of Rodin. In a letter to a friend of his in the Quarter, he promised to return from America early in November.

He will be glad to get back, this artist-errant who thought he would find in the mechanized life of America new inspiration for the rigid squares and angles of his art. His troubles began last January when he landed at Ellis Island. He was detained there two days because officials suspected he might become a public charge. Only the timely intervention of a friend prevented them from turning him back.

Being unknown in America, his work was ignored, and it was only recently that he managed to gain some recognition with an exhibition of 17 paintings at the Brooklyn Museum.[1] He has been living in a little apartment on 34th Street, Manhattan.

Montparnasse will be glad to receive him again. For ten years he has enjoyed her homage. There is no pretence about Tihanyi. He is far more interested in painting the soul of his subject than in the sale of his pictures. His paintings are not flattering, which may account for his unhappy experiences in America. His modesty and unflagging industry have won him countless friends on the Left Bank, among whom are Count Károlyi, the first president of Hungary.[2]

Tihanyi has been stone deaf for 25 years, but he can read the lips of anyone speaking French, German, Hungarian. In a few weeks, you will see a wistful little man intently studying the lips of the person he's with. That's Tihanyi.

1

The Left Bankers' Trust Co. is not incorporated and does not extend its favors to everyone. Its chief asset is the charming personality of Sylvia Beach whose book-shop on Rue de l'Odéon is the favored social club of the literati.[3] Men of letters have become so attached to the place that they call there for their mail, cash checks and borrow money. They usually return the money. The walls of the shop are covered with an interesting collection of photographs of the great. One set shows the evolution of James Joyce up from his pinafore days.

*
* *

1. Fourteen of Lajos Tihanyi's works were displayed at "A Group Exhibition of Paintings, Sculpture, and Drawings by American and Foreign Artists" at the Brooklyn Museum, June-October 1929.
2. Mihály Károlyi became Hungary's president on 16 November 1918. He was overthrown on 12 March 1919.
3. Sylvia Beach's shop was the important Shakespeare and Company. See her *Shakespeare and Company* (New York: Harcourt, Brace, 1959; London: Faber & Faber, 1960).

Monday, 28 October 1929, p. 4.

*
* *

Kiki was kissing all comers last Saturday night. The line formed about 9 o'clock outside of a book shop on Boulevard Raspail. When the news swept the Quarter that for 30 francs, one could get a copy of Kiki's *Memoirs*, her autograph and a kiss in the bargain, men forgot their *demis*, dates and dignity, and scampered over.[1] One snow-bearded octogenarian, who is well known in the Quarter, hobbled along to the party and came out with two books under his arm.

*
* *

Jimmie of the Falstaff would rather be a barman in Montparnasse than a banker on the Right Bank.[2] His popularity is so great that several night-clubs have offered to triple his salary if he would cross the river. But they don't know Jimmie.

Jimmie's father was an actor. So was Jimmie, but when he stopped the show one day with a show of his own behind the scenes that eliminated

2

about half of the male cast, his family decided to let him have his way. He became a prize fighter. His name was Kid Comet after that, and he was one of the toughest little battlers that ever crawled through the ropes. He must have loved the ring, because he gave her every tooth in his head. Now he hasn't a tooth he can call his own.

In 1920, an artist friend brought him to the Quarter. The denizens liked his sympathetic nature, and there was something about their colorful way of living that appealed to him. He became a barman and, since then, has served drinks behind nearly every well-known bar on the Left Bank. He reigns at the Falstaff with the intuitive wisdom that makes the perfect barman. When drinking gets a little heavy, and war is in the air, Jimmie accomplishes more with the soothing syrup of his smile and a few deprecatory words than is usually effected by the punitive methods of a troop of garçons.

The Quarter is Jimmie's sesame. If you ask him whether he ever intends to leave it, he'll smile shyly and change the subject. If the gilded crannies across the river think they can lure him from Montparnasse, they don't know Jimmie.

*
* *

1. Kiki was Alice Prin. Bald refers to *Les Souvenirs de Kiki* (Paris: Broca, 1929).
2. Jimmie was James Charters.

Monday, 4 November 1929, p. 4.

*
* *

The Vorticists, Dadaists, Surrealists and other believers in bigger, better and stranger art are going to get a shock when Hilaire Hiler opens his exhibit of 20 paintings at the Galerie Zborowski on the 22nd of this month. The reason is that Mr. Hiler is one [step]—if not several steps—ahead of them. After years of strenuous application he has evolved a new technique known as Neonaturism and it is said to be more advanced than any of the other "isms." The vanguardists are now in danger of finding themselves lagging near the rear, but perhaps they will console themselves with the thought that after all it is the most original place for the vanguard to be.

It should not be presumed, however, that Mr. Hiler's work has nothing but its originality to recommend it. Ezra Pound, with wonted enthusiasm and unwonted clarity—in all due respect, Mr. Pound—says of him, "Here is a

3

man who has discovered a method that retains the abstract principles of modern art, and brings them closer to life."[1]

*
* *

Hot off the press comes *The Black Christ*, Countee Cullen's third volume of poetry.

Cullen is seldom seen on the Happy Highway. He prefers the seclusion and detachment of his studio out Montsourris way, where he has been living for the past year, as the guest of Julien Green, that popular Montparnassian. Cullen hails from Harlem and is generally acknowledged as one of her most brilliant progeny. He's a fine fellow, this poet, with none of the grating peccadilloes that usually mark a man of letters. He is extremely modest in manner and speech, yet he has every reason to think well of himself, for ever since his first poem, "To a Brown Girl," appeared in *Bookman* years ago, his grip on recognition has become increasingly secure, culminating in his being granted the Guggenheim Fellowship, which is a rare distinction in America.[2]

The Black Christ, published by Putnam in London, and Harper's in the States, is a narrative poem treated highly subjectively on the subject of lynching. *Color* was printed in 1925 and *Copper Sun* two years later.[3]

Eric Walrond, another Guggenheim scholar, is living with Countee Cullen. He is hard at work on his next novel, which we hope will be as interesting as *Tropic Death*, published a couple of years ago.[4] Walrond, who was born in Georgetown, British Guiana, has traveled extensively, but considers the Left Bank as the bright spot of the cultural world. "Its traditions and literary associations," he says, "stimulate the best efforts in one. Here one can find variety or peace." When Walrond isn't busy at work, he stops in, on occasion, at the Dôme where he meets a number of his friends.

Gene Tunney has been weaned from Shakespeare, Shaw and Thornton Wilder—at least long enough to get acquainted with modern literature as the term is understood on the Left Bank. He has been exposed to *This Quarter*—published here by E. W. Titus—and according to those in London who witnessed the experiment, the inoculation took.

Mr. Titus, who is pleased to consider the Battling Bookworm among his subscribers, announces that the second issue of his magazine will appear Nov. 10.[5] Paul Valéry, Claude McKay, Countee Cullen and Robert McAlmon are among the contributors.

*

1. Source unknown.
2. Bald probably refers to "To a Brown Boy," *Bookman*, 58 (November 1923), p. 245.
3. Countee Cullen, *The Black Christ* (New York & London: Harper, 1929); *Color* (New York & London: Harper, 1925); *Copper Sun* (New York & London: Harper, 1927).
4. Eric Walrond, *Tropic Death* (New York: Boni & Liveright, 1926). Walrond published no other novel.
5. E. W. Titus edited *This Quarter* from 1929 until 1932. The first number is that of July-August-September 1929; the second, October-November-December 1929.

Monday, 11 November 1929, p. 4.

Montparnasse is all worked up about M. Georges Omer's exposé of the great Left Bank Boxer movement said to have been organized to keep the Foreign Devils out of Montparnasse and to save Europe's soul from the curse of American culture. When M. Omer's articles first appeared in a French daily and were then translated for the American press, it was almost as if a bombshell had been dropped in the middle of Montparnasse. Hard-boiled esthetes hinted darkly they might even read the articles if someone would lend them a paper, and several persons were so excited they forgot to pay for their drinks. It can be judged from this how great a sensation was caused. In fact the excitement was so high and so general that several serious drinkers even talked wildly of sending someone across the street to ask someone if anyone knew anyone who knew the name of M. Omer's anti-American bar.[1]

This project was finally abandoned, to the relief of timorous souls who justly pointed out that there was no telling to what lengths such a radical step might lead. One young artist sitting in front of the Select voiced the general opinion when he yawned and said, "What's all the shooting for, anyway? That guy Omer must have gotten a few pernods around here that back-fired. He must be angry or something."

This statement aroused great enthusiasm and several people sitting near the speaker said they would have been glad to pay for his drinks if they had not left their small change at home.

New movements in poetry, music or cocktail-shaking are the conventional thing, but when a poet turns philanthropist, he hops out of bounds: he treats us to a sensation. E. W. Titus, the publisher of *This Quarter*, announces that Richard Aldington, the Imagist, offers 2500 francs for the best poetry appearing in that magazine. Perhaps Mr. Aldington grew sentimental over his principal character in the recently published *Death of a Hero*.[2] At any rate, the poets have begun to sharpen their pencils and go to work, for no bard is blind to the fact that a nest egg loaded with franc-pieces should lure the fairest Muses into a cold attic for the rest of the winter.

Ludwig Lewisohn, who has achieved some recognition as a novelist, will probably add another plume to his bonnet when Harper's publishes his first play, *Adam*, next month.[3] There has been quite a bit of fiction written about our ancestor lately, so I asked him what sort of an Adam he was conceiving.

"A thinking, brooding Adam, something like Hamlet," was the laconic reply. I was a bit nonplussed, for I wondered what old Adam had to brood about. Mr. Lewisohn is somewhat chary with explanations, but one can hazard a guess that the popular author, who has lived in the Quarter about two years, will probably depict his brain-child as a solemn prophet nursing his complexes and shaking his head in wonder at the vagaries of his descendants.

The peculiar spirit of the Latin Quarter that makes it the focal point for the accredited and discredited alike, will be preserved in oil by Rowley Smart, the prominent English painter who has lived in the Quarter for the greater part of the last 25 years. He is preparing 30 canvases depicting the types and moods of Montparnasse and will show them in the spring. Rowley has exhibited in virtually every art capital in Europe. He is so well thought of in England that the British Government Galleries have bought four of his paintings this year, and Augustus John considers him the greatest English painter today. Consequently the preservation of the lights and shadows of life in the colony today is in capable hands.

When Rowley is not at work, he is usually seen at the Falstaff or the Dingo. If anyone thinks he lacks imagination or a vigorous, Rabelaisian wealth of humor, he should drop in at the latter bar and study the cosmic, jingoistic, adjective-defying piece of Impressionism that covers one wall. It takes Ruth about half an hour to introduce one to all of the personalities depicted. Rowley painted that last year, and is now making a sketch of the Dingo itself. He's a merry fellow and easily recognizable by the rainbow-hued scarf around his neck.

*
* *

1. Georges Omer's exposé is "A la recherche d'une société secrète contre l'esprit américain," *Paris-Midi*, 8 November 1929, p. 2. The *Chicago Tribune* (European edition) carried it the next day on p. 2, with the following translated from Omer's French: the spirit behind the anti-American society is "a tall and elegant woman often seen in the company of a man with a prophetic name who owns a bar named after the novel of a young writer who is no longer young."
2. Richard Aldington announces the prize in *This Quarter*, 2.2 (October-November-December 1929), p. 349. Aldington, *Death of a Hero* (London: Chatto & Windus, 1929; New York: Covici Friede, 1929).
3. Ludwig Lewisohn, *Adam: A Dramatic History in a Prologue Seven Scenes and an Epilogue* (New York & London: Harper, 1929).

Monday, 18 November 1929, p. 5.

*
* *

Ezra Pound writes from Rapallo:

> Shocking lack of correlation, not to notice the connection between Mr. Aldington's action (the poet's prize gift) and the "movement" discovered or advertised by Mons. Georges Omer.
> Reverentially Yrs.
>
> E.P.

If Mr. Pound were a minor poet, one might conclude that he is concerned with the rhyme scheme of "alarmist" and "altruist." But that evidently was not his interest. He should be accused of shocking inconsistency for he tells us in his "Ballad for Gloom" that "the ending is the same."[1] Therefore why bother about correlations? In his communication from Rapallo to this column, Mr. Pound is guilty of the shocking error of misspelling the tabulator's name, for which he is forgiven. Anyone living in the Quarter should overlook the inconsistencies and errors of a poet who writes:

> Sing we for love and idleness
> Naught else is worth the having.[2]

*

1. Ezra Pound included "Ballad for Gloom" in his first book, A Lume Spento (Venice: Printed for the author by A. Antonini, 1908).
2. These are the opening lines of Pound's "An Immorality" (1912). It appears in Ripostes (London: Swift, 1912; Boston: Small, Maynard, 1913).

Monday, 25 November 1929, p. 4.

When the Queen of Montparnasse appeared before the Club du Faubourg last week and thanked her audience for their warm reception of her book and herself, she had the able support of her court jester. He is Henri Broca, the cosmopolitan, urbane artist-wit who looks like a banker and draws with a poignard—that is, his caricatures prick his subjects with uncompromising satire.

Broca comes from that region of France commonly referred to as *Midi moins le quart*. This may account for the volubility of his speech. In the same breath, he talks about Rio de Janeiro, his 40-day voyage to the Antilles and his first caricature of a horse, sketched at the age of five. He has been a sailor, journalist, actor, stage-manager and what not. Now he is one of the foremost *arrivés* of the Latin Quarter.

Broca's book, *Viens t'en à Montparnasse!*, was one of the Quarter's best sellers two years ago, despite the fact that it was written and illustrated in eight days.[1] His caricatures of Tihanyi, Ollé, Jensen, Chambon, etc. are almost classic.

It is indisputable that Broca is largely responsible for the ascending star of Kiki. He launched her book, he taught her to paint; he boosted her, inspired her, and developed her eye for publicity.

Last summer, at the Bobino, the *grandes vedettes* of Montparnasse, with

Broca in the lead, elected Kiki the Queen of Montparnasse. Last week, before the forum of the Club du Faubourg he read choice extracts from her *Souvenirs*.[2]

About a fortnight ago, Kiki and Mistinguett were espied in the Coupole by a young man and his fiancée.

"Aren't they a remarkable pair?" said the young man after a long and minute scrutiny. "They look like mother and daughter."

"Which one looks like the daughter?" asked the fiancée in a scratching soprano.

Michael Arlen is petulant over his recent vacation at the American Hospital. "A trifling nuisance," he calls it. "An interruption in my work." He is back in his studio on Rue Masseran. Mr. Arlen was staring moodily into a blazing log-fire, while he alternately played with his dog, Sonny, and complained of his enforced holiday.

The scene of his next novel will be laid in New York.[3] It is the story of the marriage of an American lady and a Frenchman, told from a French point of view. The book will probably be out next summer. I asked him for a single descriptive adjective and the answer was, of course, "Cosmopolitan."

The Bird of God has taken a meteoric flight, for Virginia Hersch, formerly unknown, is now hailed as one of the literary "finds" of today. The book, dealing with the character and times of El Greco, has a power and beauty that call to mind Feuchtwanger.

Mrs. Hersch is seriously considering another interpretive novel, built around St. Teresa of Avila.[4] She will have more detailed information about the famous nun, whose startling volume of memoirs has a Freudian content. The author is a San Francisco woman who has lived in the Quarter for the past ten years.

*
* *

Nina Hamnett is coming back to the Quarter after having lived in England for three years. Nina is the kind of girl that men turn to look at and admire, but they'll have to turn fast for rumor has it that her present companion is a prize-fighter. She is a clever cartoonist and was liberally lauded for her amusing illustrations of Sitwell's *Statues of London*.[5]

*
* *

1. Henri Broca, *T'en fais pas, viens à Montparnasse!* (Paris: S. G. I. É., 1928). No copy of this book is known to exist. My information is from the card catalogue of the New York Public Library, whose copy is missing.
2. See p. 3, n. 1.
3. Michael Arlen's next novel was *Men Dislike Women* (London: Heinemann, 1931; Garden City, N.Y.: Doubleday, Doran, 1931).
4. Virginia Hersch, *Bird of God: The Romance of El Greco* (New York & London: Harper, 1929). Her next book was *Woman under Glass: Saint Teresa of Ávila* (New York & London: Harper, 1930). Bald refers to Leon Feuchtwanger (1884-1958), a German novelist and playwright.
5. Which boxer, if any, accompanied Nina Hamnett to Paris cannot be determined. For an account of her association with boxers, see Hamnett, *Is She a Lady?* (London: Allan Wingate, 1955), pp. 49-52, 84, 95-96. She discusses a trip to Paris on pp. 42, 44. Hamnett's line drawings appear in Osbert Sitwell's *The People's Album of London Statues* (London: Duckworth, 1928).

Monday, 2 December 1929, p. 5.

"Murder, Murder" ought to find a publisher, for here is a novel saturated and coated with Surrealism.[1] It's full of fancy, wild imaginings and a lot of things that should commend it to lovers of the ultra-violet in modern literature. It's a psychic mystery story more sinister than Cagliari [*sic*], in which the killed, killer and man-hunter are the same person.

The Dôme has contributed most of the characters who are easily recognized in this surrealistic prose that makes Baudelaire, Villiers and Huysmans read like *Alice in Wonderland*. No publisher has been found, but one chapter was recently printed in a crusading local magazine, wherein we read the following: "I am no fish, tin can, to describe a struggle under water. . . . She drifts slowly, slowly, and comes mechanically with roots and scenery."[2]

The author is Laurence Vail, who looks like a Viking but is really an American born in Paris. Vail is a double-barreled Surrealist, for he is also an artist. The second barrel dates back 10 years when Dadaism became the latest in art. Vail added an easel to his equipment and launched a movement of his own called Gagaism. Gaga and Dada fought it out until they both passed into the limbo of the antiquated.

Visiting Vail's studio on Avenue du Maine should be a process, not a single experience. Anyone coming the first time should enter quickly, look and run. Thus he may become accustomed to the macabre feel of the place. There are sketches of feathered trees, worms with human heads, heads without necks, houses with smiling profiles, strange shell fish flying past comets and other phenomena. Vail will solemnly assure you that the pictures have a nightmare significance. I once pointed to a particular work of art suspended from the arm of a human skeleton jangling from the somewhat remote ceiling, and assured the artist that it was one of the most unusual things there. Vail beamed all over.

"Sindbad did that one," he said.

"Who is Sindbad?"

"Sindbad is my six-year-old boy," said Vail. "He is a Surrealist, too."

The Great American Novel has not yet been written although the auricles [sic] of Americana have been examined and reported countless times. But the job might be accomplished by an artist. There is probably no painter in the Quarter more qualified than Hilaire Hiler, who has proved his worth not only as an artist, but also as ethnologist and writer. Hiler intends to spend two years in the States recording on canvas slices of American life and habits. The cycles of labor, amusement, religion, sports, etc., are to be correlated into a representative panorama. The work will be brought back here and exhibited in London, Berlin and Paris.

Hiler's present exhibit at the Galerie Zborowski is eliciting considerable comment in the Quarter, especially since his Neonaturism is the most recent fire-brand in the art world. Ezra Pound thinks it's *the* thing and Ezra should know. A number of prominent figures are visiting Hiler's exhibit in "Painters' Alley" daily. The show will run until December 22.

Paul Morand is often seen at the Students' and Artists' Club these days. He is accumulating material for a forthcoming novel concerning the American attitude towards France.

M. Morand rivals H. G. Wells in imagination, for in his "Night at Putney," the extraordinary Habib Halabi "conquers melancholia by electromagnetism and halitosis by idododes." In his next book, the author might tell Americans in America how to conquer a yen for bad gin.

11

It is evident that the creator of the exotic "Love Powders" and the sensuous "Night in Babylon" disregards the precepts of his brain-children, for at Bill Widney's party last Monday, he declined a proffered cigarette and excellent wine, explaining that he neither smokes nor drinks.[3]

For years, Cheever Dunning has lived in his "Bird Cage" on Notre Dame des Champs. His quarters look as precarious as a house on a bamboo stick. But the poet is an Orientalist and his is the philosophy of repose. He can slump before his little coal burner for hours without wasting a word or gesture. Yet there is an aura of peace and quiet about the man that may make one envy his detachment.

Hyllus, a dramatic poem, was published in 1912; *Rococo,* a narrative work, in 1925; and *Windfalls,* a collection of short lyrics, was brought out last year.[4] As a poet, Dunning is an experimenter, constantly scanning the literary horizon for new forms. He is a student of witchcraft and Arabian literature. He is seldom seen at the Dôme; he prefers to hug his coal-burner, read the Upanishads, and dream. Deprecating rumors notwithstanding, there are a few dreamers left in the Quarter, sincere poets and artists . . . and there always will be. Dunning comes from Michigan, studied at Harvard, and will remain on the Left Bank until the "Bird Cage" collapses, which probably means, for the rest of his days.

*
* *

Sailors Don't Care is a novel written by Edwin M. Lanham, a Texas boy who returned to the States last Saturday, after having lived in the Quarter about three years. The book was published by Contact Co. It will have to remain behind because the author's account of his adventures at sea is so realistic that it was barred from the States. However, the entire first edition was sold out. It appears that all of Mencken's anti-Comstock ballyhoo can't remedy this situation. Lanham's grandfather was a former Governor of Texas.[5]

A sculptor's troubles may sometimes be reckoned in kilos. Ben Bufano, working on a statue of St. Francis of Assisi for San Francisco, constructed a model weighing 30 tons. According to French law, that's ten tons too much for transportation. The Golden Gate will have to wait until the law is made more flexible and stretched a bit for art's sake.[6] Bufano is living at Paul Manship's studio.

*

1. Laurence Vail, *Murder! Murder!* (London: Peter Davies, 1931).
2. Vail published "Murder Murder" in *transition*, 16/17 (June 1929), pp. 108–19. Bald quotes from pp. 112, 111.
3. Paul Morand's forthcoming novel was probably *Champions du monde* (Paris: Grasset, 1930). The stories "The Night at Putney" and "The Night in Babylon" are in Morand's *Closed All Night* (London: Chapman, 1924; New York: Seltzer, 1925). Bald quotes incorrectly from "The Night at Putney," p. 171. The collection originally appeared as *Fermé la nuit* (Paris: Nouvelle revue francaise, 1923). "Love Powders" is in Morand's *East India and Company* (New York: Boni, 1927).
4. Ralph Cheever Dunning, *Hyllus* (London: Lane/Bodley Head; New York: Lane, 1910); *Rococo* (Paris: Titus, 1926); *Windfalls* (Paris: Titus, 1929).
5. Edwin M. Lanham, *Sailors Don't Care* (Paris: Contact Editions, 1929). Samuel Willis Tucker Lanham served as governor of Texas from 1903 to 1907.
6. Ben Bufano stored his twelve-ton sculpture of St. Francis of Assisi in Paris until 1955. In June of that year it arrived in San Francisco; it was dedicated, in October, at the St. Francis Church, at the intersection of Montgomery Avenue and Vallejo Street.

Monday, 3 February 1930, p. 6.

*
* *

Ridicule is the easiest defense in the world, and people who are inclined to think that Gertrude Stein is a little scrambled or a charlatan, should never lose sight of the fact that many years ago, she was one of the star pupils of William James at Radcliffe, that she went through the whole gamut of science, philosophy, psychology and even medicine, that she was conversant with *Hamlet* at the age of eight, that she was a star performer at Johns Hopkins a few decades ago, etc. Wyndham Lewis classifies her with Anita Loos and refers to her as a self-conscious stutterer, but Gertrude Stein sits back and smiles, casually remarking that Mr. Lewis is British and that his attack is intrinsically British propaganda against great American writers. After 25 years in her famous apartment on the Rue de Fleurus just off the Boulevard Raspail, Miss Stein will not budge an inch. Some day, she declares, she will be understood. She is now past fifty, a little patrician-looking woman with a calm, easy manner and voice and an icy contempt for all of her critics.

"I am going to save the sentence," she said, one day at a tea. "Sentences should be word symphonies. They may be compared to a well undefiled."

"A bottomless well or one with a false bottom?" said one of the tea-drinkers.

She ignored him. "People are lazy-minded. That's why they don't understand me. My work is simple but unfamiliar."

After the tea, the little party adjourned to Miss Stein's apartment. The room is hung with many cubistic and impressionistic paintings, some of them from the brush of Picasso who has been a great friend of the valiant warrior. Gertrude decided to read an extract from "A Long Gay Book": "Loving is loving and being a baby is something. Having been a baby is something. Not having been a baby is something that comes not to be anything, and that is a thing that is beginning. Having been a baby is something, having been going on being existing. Being a baby is something."[1]

"How do you like it?" asked the famous author, shutting the book.

"Gertrude," said one of her braver friends, "you not only save the sentence, but you make it live forever."

*
* *

1. Bald quotes, not entirely correctly, from Gertrude Stein, "A Long Gay Book," *Dial*, 83.3 (September 1927), p. 236. Stein later included this piece in *Matisse Picasso and Gertrude Stein* (Paris: Plain Edition, 1933; Barton, Berlin, Millerton: Something Else Press, 1972).

Monday, 17 February 1930, p. 2.

*
* *

Bulletin:—Two friends, walking along the Boulevard, entertained each other and the rest of the promenaders with an endurance kiss. It started near the Falstaff and held until they came in front of the Coupole bar, where they were greeted by the little flower girl. Broca bought a flower, pinned it, and he and Kiki went inside.

Kiki's admirers might be interested in learning that her *Souvenirs* has been translated into English by Samuel Putnam and will be brought out in a few weeks by E. W. Titus, publisher of *This Quarter*. Ernest Hemingway wrote an amusing introduction. He considers Kiki's autobiography the best human document since the publication of Cummings' *Enormous Room*.[1]

*
* *

Ezra Pound writes from Rapallo: "You can describe me as receiving one sheet of my *Cavalcanti* a month and groaning that the neo-Thomists whom it was intended to annihilate, will all be dead and buried before the book is out, and that the surrealists will all be in the French Academy before I finish correcting the proofs."[2] Poor Ezra. This is getting to be a hell of a world.

*
* *

1. See p. 3, n. 1, and p. 5, n. 5. E. W. Titus published *Kiki's Memoirs*, translated by Samuel Putnam and with an introduction by Ernest Hemingway, in 1930. e. e. cummings, *The Enormous Room* (New York: Boni & Liveright, 1922; London: Cape, 1928).
2. Ezra Pound refers to his edition of the complete works of Guido Cavalcanti that the Aquila Press began in London in 1929. The firm failed before publishing Pound's manuscript.

Monday, 3 March 1930, p. 2.

*
* *

One gigantic figure who understands and condones the peccadilloes of the "wastrels" who spend most of their time on the terraces, is Ford Madox Ford. The aimless tribe whom Gertrude Stein called "the lost generation" has always been considered by the British author a social force, a regiment from whose ranks occasionally springs a giant big enough to take the world by the ears and spank new rhythms into the dull mass. Ford is leaving for New York after a brief stay on the Riviera. He will be missed especially by the younger literati who haunted his apartment on Rue Vaugirard for guidance and encouragement. He never tired of pointing from his window to the innumerable houses in which great masterpieces were written or painted. He has often asserted that from his window might be seen 116 chimney-tops beneath each of which a great work has been written.

Many of us recall the long walks we took in groups through the Bois de

Boulogne on moonlit June nights, with Ford leading the way, talking, always talking about everything imaginable and especially about himself. We would listen to his quiet discourses about what he told Henry James, what he told Conrad, how he cooks a fancy dish, how he began his career, the speeches he made during the war, the athlete he was in his younger days before he had asthma, the number of authors he had befriended, and all other manner of topics which were of especial interest to Ford.

And the memorable dances at some *bal musette*. Ford would hire a hall and invite his friends to dance their literary cares away. He was a graceful dancer himself, and his huge, bland bulk would wander over the smooth floor while some young poetess half his size would dance with him, perspiring and happy when it was over. When the accordian would screech its strongest notes, Ford's jaw would woggle amiably in time with the music. He was a great figure.

Ford's library is not large, but one was always impressed when he brought out volume after volume inscribed to him. Many of the best living writers of today have dedicated their work to this great monitor of letters. He values them so highly that most of the literature has been safely stowed away in a private vault. On the fly-leaf of each of the books, one reads words of affectionate regard for the man who has been called the Leviathan of Montparnasse. They are still significant, but there is one that has so impressed itself on my susceptible nature that in my last delirious moments, it shall be conjured up with the force of an oath but with the fragrance of a daisy. Here it is: "To Ford Madox Ford, who has often said he is a great author and critic and thanking him for both."

*

Monday, 7 April 1930, p. 2.

*
*   *

As a publication pointing at sophistication, the magazine *This Quarter* should satisfy the fastidious. The list of contributors is headed by Paul Valéry, whose minute analysis of Stendhal's brain and character is cleverly translated. There is a number by Pierre Minet called "Overture," which is a painstaking and almost painful attempt at self-analysis. We read that "Nothing interests me so much as myself" and "Having nothing better to do, I pretend being cuckoo, hum songs of sadness or, in public conveyances, shout 'Great gun!'"

There is a poem by A. S. J. Tessimond which ends with: "two cranes do a hundred-ton tango against the sky." Quite modern. The prize-winning Julien Green has an offering called "Christine," an admirable psychological study, probably the best in the magazine. There is a hair-raiser by Norah Hoult, a marital tragedy about a brooding husband, neurasthenic wife and three or four planes of horror, including murder and betrayal. The publisher also contributes an unpretentious, learned essay entitled: "The Function of the Translator of Poetry."[1]

*
* *

1. Bald refers to *This Quarter*, 2.3 (January-February-March 1930). The contributions he mentions are these: Paul Valéry, "Stendhal," pp. 379–418; Pierre Minet, "Overture," pp. 421–34 (the quotations are from p. 432); A. S. J. Tessimond, "La Marche des Machines," p. 509, and "Chaplin," p. 510; Julien Green, "Christine," pp. 463–76; Norah Hoult, "The Way He Went," pp. 517–35; Edward W. Titus, "The Function of the Translator of Poetry," pp. 493–502.

Monday, 21 April 1930, p. 2.

A blond woman, serene as an abbess of the Middle Ages, is often seen walking in the vicinity of the Place de l'Odéon. She always wears the same habit: a severe gray coat and dress, a white silk scarf and a thin border of blue edging her white cuffs. A cape-like mantle, buttoned securely to her chin, completes the impression of a military uniform. The woman is Mlle. Adrienne Monnier, whose bookshop in the Rue de l'Odéon is often visited by almost every American writer who comes to Paris.[1]

"For many years," Mlle. Monnier tells her friends, "I have worn clothes of this simple design. I have escaped the tyranny of dressmakers."

"Why those particular colors?" she is frequently asked.

"Clothes should be symbolic of a woman's temperament," she explains. "Gray is the color of cities and structures. It represents activity and strength. Blue is the symbol of tranquility and white of the pure state of spiritual grace. These clothes are my personality and I shall always wear them." It would seem to an observer that her clear hazel eyes and rosy complexion are symbolic of good health and digestion.

On the walls of the interesting bookstore are hung an assortment of photographs and sketches of the literary luminaries of today. Many of them are

American, for Mlle. Monnier is a devotee to modern American literature. She speaks highly of Sandburg, Anderson, Hemingway, Fitzgerald and others, and is responsible for much of their work being translated into French.[2]

"American writers are renewing the art of narration," she says. "Their work has vigor and their influence is spreading rapidly. There is real genius in America." Much of our modern prose was translated and printed in her *Le Navire d'Argent*, a magazine similar to the *Seven Arts* that ran in New York. It is now defunct.

Mlle. Monnier is publishing the first definitive translation of *Ulysses*, and we learn that the French reading public are devouring the work.[3] Joyce sometimes drops in and spends an agreeable hour or two with his literary friends who frequent the bookstore.

The young Frenchwoman is also a well-known writer, and her contributions to the internationally famous *Nouvelle Revue Française* are greatly admired.[4] She writes under the name of J. M. Sollier. The liberality of her philosophic and literary ideas, coupled with a warm and unaffected personality, attracts all thinking Americans who can appreciate the significance of the blue, gray and white of a creative woman.

1. Adrienne Monnier's bookshop was La Maison des Amis des Livres, 7, rue de l'Odéon.
2. See, for example, Ernest Hemingway's "The Undefeated," translated by Georges Duplaix and published as "L'invincible," *Le Navire d'Argent*, 2 (March 1926), pp. 161-94. Monnier published this periodical in 1925 and 1926.
3. Bald refers to *Ulysse* (Paris: A. Monnier/La Maison des Amis des Livres, 1929).
4. See, for example, Monnier's "Cirque," *La Nouvelle Revue Française*, 43 [i.e., 44].258 (March 1935), pp. 487-90.

Monday, 7 July 1930, p. 2.

Samuel Putnam is the father of a new Kiki. He prays that God and Kiki forgive him but what he did was necessary for the good of Montparnasse. Before Putnam, Kiki was rapidly spreading into a legend. Now, after his experience, she belongs to the ages. Let's say 29.

All we know is this. After a brief acquaintance, Putnam decided to translate Kiki's *Memoirs* into English. It was only fair to her. In his introduction, he said: "The problem is not to translate Kiki's text, but to translate Kiki. To be able to do this, one must have the feel of Kiki."[1] Others have felt this macrocosmic personality and been glad. Putnam put English on it, as they say, and here is what happened.

On the terrace of the Dôme and the Coupole, in the quiet studios of artists and writers, at the Deux Magots and on the Right Bank, everyone is discussing the English version of Kiki's *Memoirs*. They tell me it is the most daring event of the year. There is no subtraction from the French version. In fact, twenty leaves were added to the mulberry bush. Small wonder then that this book is creating an unparalleled sensation.

In his lusty introduction Ernest Hemingway says: "If you ever tire of books written by present day lady writers of all sexes, you have a book here written by a woman who was never a lady at any time." Again he says: "She certainly dominated that era of Montparnasse more than Queen Victoria ever dominated the Victorian era."[2] They say it is impossible to sit all afternoon on the terrace of the Dôme without seeing Kiki or hearing mention of her name.

And yet Kiki, the focal interest of Montparnasse, was becoming unreal. Tourists sitting in the crowd would stare at the lady (or woman) and play guessing games as to her past. Putnam came along and whispered in her ear. She consented to have her book translated providing it be unclipped. Unclipped it is, and while some Americans are shocked, others are whistling like school-boys, for the book reveals a world wherein life is as simple as breathing. Above all, it is a document of Montparnasse. It suggests to orderly people new possibilities.

"Kiki's style," says the translator's introduction, "is the most subtle that I know. At rare moments, you think of a remote sort of Anita Loos flapper, but the next moment, you banish the thought as sacrilege. I know of no other prose so hiddenly delicate, so deceptively nuanced—not even *Fanny Hill*."[3] The fact that Putnam was serious and not kidding is revealed as one turns the pages and guesses their content. Like the carefully veiled insinuations of *Fanny Hill*, so subtly concealed that college boys tear their jerseys from end to end while guessing.

The real value of the book, however, is its searching penetration into the character of Montparnasse. The intuitive reactions of Kiki to the individuals and crowds of this world are more revealing than the thundering and fictionized word-excursions of the literary gentry. Her experiences as a model, ammunition worker, house maid, bar maid, and other professions are told without emotion or exaggeration. The chapter entitled "Love Wakes" is of universal interest.[4]

Kiki has met them all. Foujita, Broca, Kisling, Pascin, Man Ray and other astral bodies are her playmates. Years ago the vedettes crowned her Queen of Montparnasse. Like Catherine of Russia, her lovers were frequent. But I never had a hand in it. Never was she daunted by the magnitude of her courtiers.

Here is an account of her first contact with Jean Cocteau. "He came to have his photograph made. He had put on a pair of woolen gloves colored red, white, and black. I thought at first that he must have come to have his gloves photographed!"[5]

A number of Kiki's paintings decorate the bookshop of Edward W. Titus, just around the corner from the Dôme. It was Titus who decided to publish the translation of her book. In his introductory note, he says, "It was from me that Kiki received the first suggestion to write them. Generous enough with promises, she always stopped short of performance."[6] Thus Titus stopped short of persuasion, but Henri Broca gave her a push and she went to work.

Putnam's job was not easy. Yet this litterateur who wrote that "all translation is a miracle," has rendered in English a translation that has them sounding gongs in Montparnasse.[7] Kiki is so satisfied that she has offered to learn English in order to translate anything Putnam writes. Although he has translated Cocteau's *Les Enfants Terribles*, Delteil's *On the River Amour*, Mauriac's *Desert of Love* and the first complete English version of Rabelais, Putnam bit his nails before he tackled this job.[8] It is no easy task to give Kiki to the American public. She was too fond of artists who loved her and proved it. Perhaps now the Americans will.

*

1. Samuel Putnam, "A Note on Kiki, St. Theresa and the Vulgate," *Kiki's Memoirs* (Paris: Titus/Black Manikin Press, 1930), p. 20.
2. Ernest Hemingway, "Introduction," *Kiki's Memoirs*, pp. 14, 12.
3. Putnam, pp. 18-19.
4. "Love Wakes," the fifth chapter of *Kiki's Memoirs*, reads as follows:
    I've noticed a lad who lives in the square, right across the way from my room. He is short and dumpy with a wicked look. I am thinking about taking him into the back room some evening and letting him make me.
    He's kissed me and loved me up, but I haven't quite got the nerve.
    Nothing happens at all, and I go back upstairs to my room, promising him that there'll be something doing some of these days.

5. Bald quotes from "Jean Cocteau," *Kiki's Memoirs*, p. 171.
6. E. W. T[itus]., "Publisher's Note," *Kiki's Memoirs*, p. 24.
7. Putnam, p. 18.
8. Putnam translated the following: Jean Cocteau, *Enfants terribles* (New York: Brewer & Warren, 1930); Joseph Delteil, *On the River Amour* (New York: Covici Friede, 1929); François Mauriac, *The Desert of Love* (New York: Covici Friede, 1929); François Rabelais, *All the Extant Works* (New York: Covici Friede, 1929).

Tuesday, 12 August 1930, p. 4.

Louise Bryant is writing a poem—"Myth of the Lady Unexplored." Two lines read:

> And there was a round absurdity
> Called the earth.

When Louise was 16, she wrote a play called *The Game*, wherein Life and Death shoot craps for the bodies of soldiers. It was the first play produced in New York by the Provincetown Players and pointedly reveals the girl's first glimpse at absurdity.[1]

Since then, she has found it all a drama and the drama absurd, but she has played it from more angles than any other woman I know. Mussolini will back me up, but first let's dispense with Eugene O'Neill.

Some years back, Louise Bryant, a girl in pigtails from San Francisco, became one of the original three directors of the Provincetown Players. The other two were George Cram Cook and Jack Reed.[2] Her energy and ability were so marked that O'Neill insisted that she act.

"Imagine," explains Louise. "They always gave me dying parts. When they put on O'Neill's *Thirst*, I was dying with two men on a raft. Every night I had to say, 'O give me one drop of water,' and then fall off the raft. Every time I fell I cracked my head against the edge of the raft, and became so disgusted that I told Gene I never wanted to die again. It was absurd."[3]

Not long after, Louise was in Russia with Jack Reed, whom she had married. Reed's *Ten Days That Shook the World* was one of the most talked-of books of the day.[4] Louise had established a reputation as a war correspondent and had been the only woman present among that tiny news brigade, one of whose number was Floyd Gibbons, who shortly after lost his famous eye. The current was swift in those days, and when the Allies attacked Rus-

21

sia, she was caught within its closed borders and was virtually a prisoner during the awful famine which lasted over a year.

Jack Reed died. Louise was alone in Russia. She was arrested and pardoned a dozen times. She was the only American war correspondent in Moscow whose news stories left the country. They were cabled around the world and her reputation was made. Doran and Company later brought out her *Six Red Months in Russia* which was followed by *Mirrors of Moscow*, published by Putnam.[5]

In the words of an American musical clown, "You ain't heard nothing yet." The life of Louise is a rush and a jump. She is one of the better artists of Montparnasse, an accredited sculptor, an accomplished pianist. For years she has worked as foreign correspondent for a number of syndicates, among them being the International News Service. She is busy now on two novels: one for Harper's, one for Liveright. Her poems have frequently appeared in *Century* and *Cosmopolitan*.[6] And—

Three or four times a week, just before the sun comes up, we are accustomed to seeing this dark-eyed dynamo clad in a military blue mantle and a black beret, pacing nervously in front of the Dôme. She is waiting for the bus that takes her to Le Bourget field. For Louise loves to fly and we understand that she flies alone. Perhaps the clouds are not absurd.

I almost forgot about Mussolini. Before Louise attacked the Duce, no correspondent could approach him. He laughed when she tried to get him.

"Women," said Mussolini, "should write about blue skies."

She tracked him for a month, learned everything about him to the number of his teeth, wrote the story, showed it to him; and her insight so astounded him that, it should be boldly stated, the Duce's respect for women may in a measure be attributed to Louise. He not only approved of the story; he signed it.[7]

For the past five years, Louise has been living in a studio adjoining a nunnery, in the Rue d'Assas. To quote Louise, the place is "absurd." Candles afford the only light at night and dark shadows shiver on the walls and ceiling. From her window she can watch the nuns walking in the garden; and sometimes at night, when the click of her typewriter ceases, Louise is in the habit of watching the shadows thrown from the candles while the nuns whisper in the garden below. The shadows fall on the ikons, silken fans, bronze images, Japanese boxes and chunks of wet clay covered by Turkish towels. Also buckets of wood and pails of tin, for there is no running water in Louise's apartment.

*
*   *

1. Louise Bryant's poem apparently was not published. *The Game* was performed in 1916, which was, technically, the Provincetown Players's second season. If Bryant wrote the play in 1916, as seems likely, she was then thirty years old. See Bryant's *The Game* in *The Provincetown Plays*, 1st ser. (New York: Frank Shay, 1916), pp. 28–42. See also Helen Deutsch and Stella Hanau, *The Provincetown* (New York: Farrar & Rinehart, 1931), p. 199.
2. Bryant, George Cram Cook, and John Reed were among the original twenty-nine members of the Provincetown Players.
3. Bryant appeared as Dancer in Eugene O'Neill's *Thirst* in 1916. She also performed that year as Margot in John Reed's *The Eternal Quadrangle*.
4. John Reed, *Ten Days That Shook the World* (New York: Boni & Liveright, 1919; London: Communist Party of Great Britain, 1926).
5. Bryant, *Six Red Months in Russia* (New York: Doran, 1918; London: Heinemann, 1919); *Mirrors of Moscow* (New York: Seltzer, 1923).
6. Bryant published no novels; she published poems in neither *Century* nor *Cosmopolitan*. Her verse appears frequently in *The Masses*: "From the Tower," 8.9 (July 1916), p. 22; "A Wish," 8.11 (September 1916), p. 26; "Six Poems," 8.12 (October 1916), p. 20; "Lost Music," 9.3 (January 1917), p. 43; "Sensations," 9.6 (April 1917), p. 37; "Dark Eyes," 9.9 (July 1917), p. 28.
7. Bryant's story on Mussolini, datelined Rome, 25 January 1923, appears under the headline "Mussolini Relies upon Dated Efficiency to Restore Italy" in the *New York American*, 28 January 1923, sec. 52 ("March of Events" section), p. 1.

Tuesday, 19 August 1930, p. 4.

Michael Arlen has met the Countess.

The sad sophisticate, who lives near the Gare Montparnasse, stepped into the Falstaff a few nights ago. Three tables to his right the Countess was staring dreamily into her coffee cup. He looked. She looked. They chuckled in a dignified way. Michael Arlen stroked his moustache and the Countess approached.

"So you are Michael Arlen?" she said. Her voice was heavy with frustration. The writer nodded.

"You sweet person," said the Countess. "How you must have suffered! But tell me something. This is impossible! Really, this must be impossible! You couldn't have written *These Charming People*.[1] Why my dear, I've heard you speak and you can't even talk Oxford English!" The writer sighed, the listeners sighed, Jimmie sighed, Joe sighed, the *patron* sighed.

"Don't disturb the gentleman," said Joe.

"Oh!" said the Countess. Her fragile voice g. ew as she spoke. "He looks like a sweet what-not and he appears to be so unhappy. He is a floundered soul. A babe in the woods. We are all babes in the woods. All of us. But I don't care. Why should anyone care? Now, Joe, give Mr. Babe in the Woods another drink. He understands me for he has written about me in every one of his books whether he knows it or not." The Countess was rattling with emotion as she returned to her table.

Michael Arlen smiled like Menjou as he finished his drink.

*
* *

1. Michael Arlen, *These Charming People* (London: Collins, 1923; New York: Doran, 1924).

Tuesday, 2 September 1930, p. 4.

*
* *

Gasping for breath is tiresome, which explains the present desertion of Montparnasse. Most of the citizens have gone south to the Riviera. Down in Cannes, I hear that A. Lincoln Gillespie was finally caught by the limelight which he has been assiduously avoiding for the last ten years.

Last Tuesday, Link made a speech at the Chateau Madrid in Cannes. The subject was "Joyce-yen." Anyone who has heard of Joyce has heard of Link. He is always a whole jump ahead of the Surrealists and some of his work has burned the pages of the late *transition*.

The many Montparnassians who have drifted toward Cannes persuaded Mr. Lyle, the manager of the Chateau Madrid, to put on a Gillespie show. Lyle, an old Parnassian whose big black hat and long sideburns are familiar here, broke the conventional precedent and permitted the show.

While the lanterns glowed and the night birds trilled and the bats flew in all directions, Link mounted the platform of the open air night club and, unfolding a tablecloth which held his notes, began his speech. It sounded more formal than Joyce himself. Everyone applauded but no one knew what he was talking about, because words are juicy things and Link is capable of squirting the juice with more abandon than most of his contemporaries.

Peggy Hopkins Joyce happened to be there. Peggy is living in Cap d'Ail, about 35 kilometers from Cannes. A committee had persuaded her to come to the lecture.

When it was all over Peggy remarked: "I don't know what that person is talking about, but if he is talking about me, why don't he come out and say it plain?"

The Domites know Link as the author of "Amerikaka" and "Music Starts a Geometry."[1] He used to come around here with a supply of cheese in his pocket. While discussing the Italian Renaissance, Venetian glassware or Dutch architecture, Link would reach in his pocket and nibble at chunks of cheese. He is capable of discussing anything in his own language, which he is constantly inventing.

Strangely enough, Link's champion and promoter at Cannes is none other than J. P. McEvoy, known as the father of the chorus girl. He is the author of *Show Girl* and three other Broadway hits. McEvoy will soon be a Montparnassian if he is not careful, despite the fact that his *Chorus Girl in Europe* is about to be published.[2]

1. A. Lincoln Gillespie, Jr., "Amerikaka Ballet," *transition*, 16/17 (June 1929), pp. 151-56; " 'Music Starts a Geometry,' " *transition*, 8 (November 1927), pp. 166-69.
2. J. P. McEvoy, *Show Girl* (New York: Simon & Schuster, 1928). McEvoy's other recent Broadway plays were *Allez-Oop!* (1927), *Americana* (1928), and *New Americana* (1928). He neither published nor produced *Chorus Girl in Europe*.

Tuesday, 9 September 1930, p. 4.

Tin Pan Alley will soon be humming new Mammy songs for poor J. P. McEvoy . . . something like:

> Mac—come back
> To Old Broadway.
> Here the flying fishes
> Make more monnay.
> Oh Mammy!

or other such sophisticated stuff. Will McEvoy bend one of his ears? Will he go back to "Old Broadway"?

The odds in Montparnasse are about even. The tall city is beginning to realize that Broadway is dangerous, but this village is fatal. The blasé of N. Y. are discovering that Montparnasse has no sophistication because it doesn't need any. Already the bat-eyed vampire has taken a few bites at J. P. Mc-Evoy. He has switched his Joyces from Peggy to Jim.

"James Joyce," he said, "is giving us new word tools."

I was deeply impressed. "What do you think of Peggy?" I asked.

"Let's talk about James," said Mac. "Our language is all wrong."

At that moment there was a rap on the door and a splendid visitor entered. She was a lovely thing of the Dixie Dugan type. She came in to borrow a book and left.

"Now," explained Mac, "you would call her 'beautiful' but Link Gillespie would call her something like 'Mammasoful.' Do you see the difference?"

His conversation was baffling. Was this the author of *Show Girl* and *Denny and the Dumb Cluck*? He repeatedly picked analogies from the Greek classics and he seemed to know his Molière. He told me stories about Broadway and a few from Lucretius. Then I asked: "What is a gold digger?"

"A girl with imagination."

"Are all chorus girls gold diggers?"

"No," said Mac. "Some are very dumb."

Broadway has dubbed him "Father of the Chorus Girl." I was brought up to believe that every chorus girl needs a "daddy," but Mac insisted that Broadway was joking. Mac is putting the finishing touches on *Show Girl in Europe*. Already he has sold the stage rights, scenario rights, magazine rights and television rights. He is not so dumb. He knows the chorus girl. More than any other man, he has unhooked their personalities for the instruction of the curious in America. According to Mac, women "from Madame Pompadour up and down have been interested in checks appeal." It is my innocent prediction that if Montparnasse doesn't really get McEvoy, he will eventually turn out *Show Girl in Montparnasse*.[1]

McEvoy always travels with Blue Boy, a young Negro who serves as his valet. Blue Boy worked in vaudeville for a number of years before McEvoy picked him up, and Right Bankers might be interested in knowing that Brick

Top once worked for Blue Boy. The kid can sing and dance, and is clever in many other ways.

Wedding bells in Montparnasse unless it's all a joke. Friday night, Ford Madox Ford told a group at Lipp's that he had just married the young Polish girl with whom he had often been seen. The word flashed around the Quarter and congratulations began to pour in on the novelist who is getting on in years but still loves to dance. On the other hand, there are many in the Quarter who insist that Ford was only joking. When we got around to his apartment Saturday morning for confirmation, the concierge told us that Ford has just left for New York and wouldn't return for a month. And so the Quarter must hold its breath for a whole month, but everyone seems to believe that the venerable Ford will have managed to spill the beans long before that time.[2]

A farewell party was thrown for George Seldes who left for America Saturday. George is one of our best *raconteurs*. He can tell very dull stories in a very interesting fashion. He left to see about publication of another book called *The Red Terror* or *The White Terror*. Anyway it had the word "terror" in it.[3] George is a great scooper. When he worked on the Pittsburgh *Leader* some years back, he scooped Halley's comet. But the rumor had been unconfirmed.

Raymond Duncan breaks into print again, this time with a law suit. After waiting a year, he discovers that MacDougall's *Isadora Duncan's Russian Days* is an "insult to the memory of my sister." The French translation has been appearing in *Gringoire*. After five numbers were printed, Duncan obtained the injunction and the case will doubtless go to court. MacDougall told me that Christine Dallies, the translator, wrote [him] that Duncan was willing to withdraw the action if conceded a certain percentage on the royalties. "There was a 'but' in it," says MacDougall.[4]

George Antheil, now in Cagnes, is preparing eight premières of his latest works. The first two will appear in London.

Report comes in that 300 copies of Samuel Putnam's translation of *Kiki* were confiscated in New York. The village queen was informed of the bad news yesterday while sharing a cracker with her little Peky on the terrace of the Coupole. Laconically and with a characteristic shrug, she remarked: "I am not losing any weight over it."

*
* *

1. See p. 25, n. 2. J. P. McEvoy, *Denny and the Dumb Cluck* (New York: Simon & Schuster, 1930). McEvoy published neither *Show Girl in Europe* nor *Show Girl in Montparnasse.*
2. Ford Madox Ford did not marry the woman.
3. George Seldes wrote no book with *terror* in the title, although he did write *Can These Things Be!* (New York: Brewer & Warren, 1931), a book about terrorism.
4. Allan Ross MacDougall and Irma Duncan, *Isadora Duncan's Russian Days* (New York: Covici Friede, 1929; London: Gollancz, 1929). Christine Dallies's French translation appears as "Les Dernières Années d'Isadora Duncan" in *Gringoire* (Paris, 1930): 11 July, pp. 1, 2, 11; 18 July, p. 11; 25 July, p. 11; 1 August p. 11; 8 August, p. 11.

Tuesday, 16 September 1930, p. 4.

Naturally, I don't know what is meant by the term "real" Quarter or "real" Montparnasse, but if there were such a spot, Gwen Le Gallienne would doubtless be sitting in the center. Very few people would know it, because Gwen would be sitting quietly and alone. Her utter indifference would mark her, as it does every night when she comes to the Select, or during the day, when she lopes with more than reasonable speed through Montparnasse traffic.

Watch her cut through that traffic. Her flannel blue suit disappears like a powder in the crowd. Such speed has conviction; it presupposes an inner swagger, a remoteness, and above all, an indifference. That's what I was trying to say in paragraph one.

This emotional condition, often attributed to inmates of Montparnasse, is not an attitude in Gwen's case. Too many people are lightly accused of attitudes. The very few who know her—and some of them are especially interesting—insist that she is incapable of insincerity. In speech, she is direct and frank, and she never talks unless she has something to say. One sentence ordinarily suffices for the dull, curious or garrulous. After that, they stay away. Her curves, too, are interesting. They are all in her voice. Listen to it five minutes and you'll like her.

Gwen's temperament rests on chaos. She is fascinated by the intangible routes of her own career. For that reason, probably, she looks poetic, as does her father, Richard. The youngest Le Gallienne is the most chaotic looking, which, in my careless opinion, is indeed a blessing, for what is poetry but chaos carefully handled?

From birth, Gwen has lived like a gypsy. Though born in Paris, her childhood was spent in the wilds of Connecticut. In a place called Tokeneke Nook, she lived in house boats, lumber camps and tree tops with her romantic father. In a moment of confidence, she recently whispered: "During those formative years, I could climb trees faster, throw a ball farther or dive deeper than any boy in the neighborhood."

As the girl grew older, culture began to sneak up on her. She was thrown in with the literati and other holy men. For a time, she lived at the home of "Uncle" Elbert Hubbard. Also with Mrs. James Huneker who was her aunt, by marriage. At the age of 13, a change came over the girl, and one day, she tremulously approached Mrs. Huneker and whispered that she had written a play called *The Dryad*. Mrs. Huneker then suggested that she study art. In a word, then, such was her education—chartless but poetic and fascinating.

Her impulses are fascinating. Very often she slips away for a lonely tramp through Brittany. One raw night last spring, a small party was crossing the Seine in a taxi. Gwen got out and disappeared. After 10 minutes, the searchers found her. She had taken a dip, fully clothed.

Some time ago, all of her paintings were exhibited in Paris and the acclamation of the critics seemed sincere. Several of her pictures are now being exhibited in America. Americans like her work. Gwen is rising in her profession as Eva has [risen] in hers. But there are complications in Gwen's make-up that no success in art will heal. I don't know what they are. Neither does she. I can only guess that she is everlastingly blown by the pleasures and penalties of a mystic nature so highly attuned that it is no longer elastic. She has been searching too long in the dark crevices.

The propulsion of such a temperament is naturally disquieting. Perhaps it is unfortunate. But then, perhaps she has genius.

Her only real companion is a Congo leopard, aged two months. It is the gift of Wellington Furlong, author of *Let 'Er Buck.* I hate that leopard and it hates me. While I was up in Gwen's studio the other night, the leopard suddenly sprang upon me and made a neat etching on my middle finger. I rushed about the room, hunting for iodine, and Gwen laughed so hard that she was shaking. I can't understand that girl.

Last Saturday, Gwen's father left his studio in the Rue Servandoni for America. He'll be back in a month. The tall, lean poet has often been remarked walking up and down his beloved Rue de Seine, where he is known to all the shopkeepers. He loves to shop, and mornings he is seen rubbing shoulders with the rest of the crowd. He throws the stuff into a black bag where it nestles with the manuscripts. A cane is always hooked on one arm.

Le Gallienne does most of his writing in the afternoon. About every two hours he takes a nap, because he has difficulty sleeping nights. He likes to make his own coffee and drinks an enormous amount of it. His studio is an eighth heaven, so to speak. It's a Paris skyscraper, eight floors above the ground. When not working, the poet spends hours gazing over the rooftops of adjoining buildings.

He smokes a corncob and his favorite dish is mince pie. His voice is high pitched but clear as a bell. His fund of anecdotes is inexhaustible. Get him to tell you stories about the pink or mauve nineties and you'll pass one of the most pleasant hours in a big while. Stories about Beardsley and Wilde and *The Yellow Book.*

His best poem—or one of his best—was *Omar Repentant.* It was a vicious attack on booze. While writing it he drank a quart of good rye. He likes to read *La Vie Parisienne* and *Le Sourire.* He likes to chuckle and he always chuckles when he reads those snappy numbers. *There Was a Ship* is a harlequinade of a novel that has enjoyed great success in America.

Sometimes Richard comes to the Select with Gwen. Poet and painter. Gwen, he says, is his favorite daughter. He likes Eva but would like her better if he knew her better. The story goes that several years ago (this was in Detroit, where Eva was playing) father and daughter were formally introduced to each other.[1]

Radclyffe Hall used to be a frequenter of the Deux Magots and the Select. She is a very blonde woman and wears her hair smack back over a determined head. Two curls drop over her forehead. She was always seen with Lady Troubridge. Both wore monocles and both used long cigarette holders. The crisp-looking Miss Hall is said to have a practical sense quite developed and is reputed to hate the idea of promiscuity. She always traveled in a limousine.

*
* *

1. Gwen Le Gallienne—the daughter of Richard Le Gallienne's third wife Irma and her first husband, the sculptor Roland Hinton Perry—was Richard's stepdaughter. Eva Le Gallienne was the daughter of Richard and his second wife, Julie Norregard. James Huneker's second wife, Clio Hinton, was Gwen's mother's sister. Irma's parents had a house at Tokeneke Park, Darien, Connecticut. Charles Wellington Furlong, *Let 'Er Buck* (New York & London: Putnam's, 1921). First published in *Cosmopolitan*, 38.1 (November 1904), pp. 43–48, Richard Le Gallienne's *Omar Repentant* was published in book form with Kennerley in New York and Richards in London in 1908. *There Was a Ship* (Garden City, N. Y.: Doubleday, Doran, 1930).

Tuesday, 23 September 1930, p. 4.

*
* *

Raymond Duncan discovers Montparnasse. The following is selected from *New-Paris-York*, his baffling monthly:

> Paris also has her Ellis Island; it is called Montparnasse. Every day one sees crowds of strangers who arrive without that culture and talent which are the necessary passport to command their entrance into the real life of Paris.

Note: You haven't seen the "real life of Paris" until you have beheld his winsome figure gliding rapidly over the pavement. His eye is stern, his hair is long and his figure is preserved in a Turkish towel, spiraling snugly until it reaches his sandals. Then it flaps if there is a wind. I never see him without offering a benediction and an assurance to my better self that beauty and its clients will prevail.

His article concludes with: "These unfortunate [sic] seek consolation as best they can seated at café tables and attempting to at least seem to be Parisians. . . ."

In all fairness, we cannot dismiss Raymond without quoting a few lines of his poetry which may lead to a better understanding:

31

O. To breathe of the wind that is blowing
And quit this living in preserved air.
A plate of beans means more
To my stomach
Than all memories or hopes.[1]

*
* *

1. Bald refers to *New-Paris-York*, 2 (September 1930). Raymond Duncan writes about Ellis Island in "Paris possède son Ellis Island," p. 1; his poem, "Take a Breath," is on p. 17.

Wednesday, 8 October 1930, p. 4.

We get wind of a monthly—*The New Review*—to be published in Montparnasse. The first number will appear promptly on January 1, 1931.

Contributors will be leading creative writers and unknowns. Here is your chance. Ideas which lead to creation are wanted. The publication proposes to be critical in the larger, philosophical sense, although all the important books of the Continent will be reviewed each month.

Current literature is running a hellish race. Different trends diverge, converge and hate each other. Trends are as panicky as people or horses. That is because guidance comes from the rear. But panics are far more stimulating than bleached ideas or aspirin tablets. *The New Review* promises to remind its readers of the monthly panic in the literary world.

The New Review will be published by Samuel Putnam, who has secured American capital for the founding of an "International journal of creative thought." Putnam is the scholar whose American version of Rabelais created so much discussion last year and whose translation of Kiki's *Memoirs* bothered the American Customs this year. He has just completed an anthology of contemporary European writers.[1]

Putnam is young and generous. There will be no hand-woven lace fringing his magazine, nor will he sprawl heavily over half the pages. The material should interest the low brow as well as the high brow, for both have their place as have the male and the female. Fusion of virility and subtlety.

Terrace discussions of the forthcoming periodical reveal an active interest in a dependable monthly. Some have been assured that it will not be a "gentlewomanly miscellany of the Victorian era." An active organ like *The New Review* should supply a definite need.

Aleister Crowley sends a card which opens with: "Yes, indeed, but whither?" It concludes with the information: "I have something better than ideas."

To really know Crowley, read his *Diary of a Drug Fiend.*[2] He knew all the combinations and was referred to as "666."

He used to parade around here with his head shaved save for the waxed forelock which Montparnassians called the "Mark of Buddha," and which he described as his "Cling-Clong." The stodgy man of 50 was frequently seen in kilties or plus fours.

He was said to have practiced black magic and addressed the devil by his first name. He boasted of his skill in sorcery, alchemy and hypnotism. Orgies were commonplace to him; he liked to create new fashions.

Oddly enough, some people believed in Crowley. They were fascinated by his flights of fancy. His bedroom, for instance, was surrounded by mirrors and this egotist could watch himself from seven angles while lying in bed.

Few people knew the source of his income, but some insisted that he received annually 300,000 francs from an estate in Scotland. His memoirs, brought out six months ago by the Manchester Press, are selling for ten dollars a copy.[3]

Crowley had some talent as a painter. One of his best works was *Three Men Carrying a Black Goat across the Snow to Nowhere*, which also proves that he was a poet.

The French Government didn't like Crowley, and so they dismissed him about a year ago. He had plenty of color, but it was a bit too garish.

1. Samuel Putnam, *François Rabelais* (London & Toronto: Cape, 1929; New York: Cape & Smith, 1929); François Rabelais, *All the Extant Works*, translated by Putnam (New York: Covici Friede, 1929). See p. 15, n. 1.
2. Aleister Crowley, *Diary of a Drug Fiend* (London: Collins, 1922; New York: Dutton, 1923).
3. Crowley, *The Spirit of Solitude* (London: Mandrake, 1929).

Tuesday, 14 October 1930, p. 4.

Staring dreamily at the frosty faces all about her on the Coupole terrace, Fernande Barrey was drinking hot tea. She had just returned from Saint-Valery-sur-Seine.

Even from a distance, the famous surromanticist looks impressive. Romance seems to pour from her large, blue eyes, the upper lids of which are painted a bluish green. Her eyebrows are bald. She shaves them to accentuate the general softness of her face.

Pushing my way through the crowd, I approached her table. On her lap rested a large bag of onions.

"Have an onion," Fernande said in her dreamy way.

I selected a small one because I don't like onions without salt. Our neighbors and the garçons were frowning. Evidently they didn't care for onions. We talked about art and life and Frank Harris. Fernande is an aborigine. Not only was she born here, but she seems to have inherited the philosophy of Bohemianism.

Then we went to Fernande's studio in the Rue Delambre. Three cats, one dog and one magpie greeted us. Two of her paintings on the wall reveal her passion for blue. Solid blue backgrounds, blue buds. Her pictures at the Galerie Zak are noted for their color schemes. Without blue pigment, Fernande would refuse to paint. Blue is the color of surromanticism.

In the studio, there is a Victrola. She turned it on, kicked off her shoes and did a buck and wing dance.

"To reduce," she explained. That is why she likes onions. Fernande weighs 70 kilos; three months ago she weighed 85 kilos; when she married Foujita in 1917, she weighed 55 kilos.

Nothing is more depressing than a woman's battle against heft. Yet Fernande is always cheerful; she is always surromantic. But it's depressing. Many years ago, a small boy became infatuated with his teacher. He wrote a long poem and prepared to deliver it at her home. When he got there, the door was open and he walked right in. There was the teacher, doing stationary running in a pair of great, pink bloomers and in her hands were a couple of rusty dumb bells. That was the end of that.

Fernande brought some red wine, and then, during a lull in the conversation, I tentatively stroked her Pouff just to see what she would say.

"You like animals, too," she said. "All animals are sacred and should be loved."

Just then Henri Broca came in. With him were Foujita and also Koyanagui. . . .

We went to the Select. Foujita told us that he expects to leave for New York on November 1. He is a mild mannered fellow with a passion for sewing machines. He spends several hours a day composing chemises or bathrobes for his models. Just to keep his nerves in order. He has just rented a large atelier in the Rue Campagne-Première.

Broca said he may start another little publication next month—a kind of Montparnasse guide book, telling people where to eat and what to drink. His famous caricatures will be the big feature, but the guide information should be serviceable to those who don't care to bother reading the bill boards plastered everywhere.[1]

Fernande told some very funny stories and the stoical Koyanagui said nothing.

Kiki came in. The Select opens its eyes. "Kiki! Kiki!" The Queen of Montparnasse smiles naturally and joins the party. She is the girl of whom Hemingway said: "She never had a room of her own."[2]

Her greeting was: "I want a revolver." She explained that she is living alone in the country and is fearful of further complications. She is living in a suburb which translated means "The Black Cow."[3] On November 15, her paintings will be exhibited at the Georges Bernheim Gallery and shortly after she will be starred in a musical revue at the Theatre Mayol. We talked and drank for a couple of hours and then everyone went home.

This Quarter, a literary publication, announces its Russian number. Among the American contributors, we find the name of the late Cheever Dunning.[4] The magazine is a quarterly.

*
* *

Louise Bryant has a black eye and a tiny scar on her nose. She was not hit by lightning or struck by a cab door. The accident occurred at the Le Bourget field. When Louise brought her plane down, the wheels stuck in the mud, jolting her against some hard object.

Before sailing for America last week, Otto Kahn, the rich New Yorker, visited Louise at her convent studio in the Rue d'Assas. The two are old friends. He took away with him Louise's last manuscript, *The Best Seller*, which the financier will try to place on Broadway.[5]

Florence Muir writes from Hollywood that Jed Kiley is not very hot in the scenario business. Jed was released and may come back to Paris. He started the popular College Inn and wrote very good stories for *The Boulevardier*.[6]

His most famous crack was: "The way to change your girl is to change your town."

That advice is not entirely adequate because flight is undignified, and wandering from town to town eventually proves wearing. If you want to change your girl, ask her permission. Just try it.

Tell her: "Sunset, into the limbo you must go." That is enough.

Your opponent will be cool and objective, as girls invariably are when their feelings are being fluttered. Above all, she will admire your courage; and by degrees, she will so stir you with her uncurbed admiration, that you will wind up by changing your mind and holding the girl. It is easier to change your mind than a habit. That's what usually happens, anyway.

*

1. Henri Broca edited and published *Paris-Montparnasse*.
2. Ernest Hemingway, "Introduction," *Kiki's Memoirs* (Paris: Titus/Black Manikin Press, 1930), p. 14.
3. Bald refers to La Vache-Noire.
4. Ralph Cheever Dunning, "The Lady in the Cellar," *This Quarter*, 3.1 (July-August-September 1930), pp. 117-120.
5. No Louise Bryant work was produced on Broadway.
6. "Ladies Prefer Argentines," *Boulevardier*, 1.3 (May 1927), pp. 9, 40, 42, 44, is Jed Kiley's first signed contribution to this Right Bank publication. He was a regular contributor through December 1929.

Tuesday, 28 October 1930, p. 4.

A bit of a thrill hits Montparnasse. There is an alert feeling in the carrefour, for we have with us now the famous Doris Carlyle, Queen of Greenwich Village.[1]

She has been a dancer, hash slinger, mule driver; and she has had five husbands. Doris has seen more of life than have most girls. She is 40 and will be 41 next January.

Ever since she had been thrown out of three convents at a tender age, the Queen has hated conventions, and preached the joys of the libido. The Villagers liked that in her and looked upon her as a discovery. They made her Queen of the whole Village and everyone was satisfied.

The Greenwich Village Queen looks interesting as she strolls along the carrefour in a blood-red beret and great, golden earrings. Her eyes, too, are golden, but when she is angry they narrow into the ominous color of her beret. Her countenance has been a bit galvanized by hard battles, but beneath it all there lurks a true Bohemian smile. She is tall and strong.

It has been many years since the famous Queen lived in Montparnasse. We were sitting at a table in the Select, and ruminating over a few beers, when I asked what were her first impressions this trip.

"How should I know?" said the Queen. "I was drunk when I arrived."

"Do you love Montparnasse?"

The Queen snorted. "Say, where do you get that stuff? Montparnasse is just a bubble blown wrong. It used to be all right but now there are no bones left in the garbage can. Just a bunch of stews hang around here and wait for the checks that never come. Talk about atmosphere! Montparnasse doesn't smell right any more. The real gang have gone forever."

"How about Greenwich Village?"

She twirled her red beret reflectively. "That's lousy, too," she said.

A little later, she said, "What do you mean by asking me these personal questions? Why, when you were running off to school and still playing with your marbles, I was a star on Broadway. Ziegfeld's Follies two years. Then to London Music Halls two more years. And even première danseuse at the Folies-Bergère in 1915. In 1917, I danced in the *Garden of Passion* at Hammerstein's Victoria, and Comstock arrested us. Maybe you didn't know, smartie, that I posed for Epstein, Jo Davidson and Rodin, and that my figure was once considered among the best in the world." She breathed deeply and then folded her hands behind her head. It wasn't bad.

The following day, I met Doris Carlyle again and we talked about the Village.

"We were a great gang," she said. "There was Floyd Dell, Dreiser, Frank Harris, Polly Holliday, Irving Berlin, Harry Kemp, Eugene O'Neill, Big Bill Holliday and a hundred others. But they've all separated."

"When you were made Queen, did they crown you?"

"And how!" said the romantic looking woman. "They gave a big Pagan Route Ball at Webster Hall. I danced as Astarte before 4,500 people and everyone was stewed to the eyeballs. Some of them were so full of snow that their noses were frozen. What a night! After they crowned me, I went into the Dance of the Seven Veils. And say! When I danced, you could hear their hearts whistle. I fooled everyone by wearing eight veils, but they didn't lose faith in me."

She became so enthusiastic that she was about to leap upon a chair and give a summary performance. The quick-witted garçon pulled all the extra chairs out of reach. After all, this is only Montparnasse.

"Then came Prohibition," sighed the Queen. "I got disgusted and beat it. When I beat it, the Village fell apart."

She went to South America.

"In South America, I had a streak of hard luck. I beat my way from Brazil to Chili, and from Chili to the Argentine. I rode in the freights or the blinds and slept in box cars. I even crossed the Andes on a mule wagon. I worked as a fireman and once as a stoker on a ship. And, would you believe it, once I was stranded on the Barbary Coast."

"Did you ever sleep in jails?" I asked.

"Of course," said the Queen. "I slept in jails about twice a week."

"Why?"

"For socking guys like you who ask too many personal questions. How do you get that way?"

I said something like "Be yourself," or "Act your age." I forget what I said. We had another beer and I didn't see the Greenwich Village Queen again until last Saturday afternoon. I visited her place in the Rue Fermat, where I discovered to my amazement that this peppery enigma was working hard at a bust.

Another woman was present and was acting as a model.

"So you are a sculptor too, I see. Such versatility!"

"Sure," the Queen said, heartily. "I love to sculpt."

She finally dismissed the model, and then became confidential.

"I am also writing my memoirs," she said. "When the book comes out in December or in January or possibly February, you're going to see the sensation of the year. My book will be so hot that you will have to wear gloves to read it. It will tell all and no one will be spared." She twirled her red beret and grinned at some object over my shoulder. It was a black cat.

"I am living a quiet and clean life these days," she said. "Me and my cat and my cigarettes. I have had plenty of battles. Some nice little hillside cottage would suit me fine. Just wait until my memoirs come out." She called the cat.

"I love my cat," she purred, stroking it gently. "Cats don't make dirty remarks. They don't tell lies. They don't gossip. They are clean and honest. Of course, my little Ruthie has her gentlemen friends, but she knows how to handle them. She's no fool."

*

1. In his columns of 22 December 1931 and 26 January 1932, Bald refers to Dolores Carlyle. If her name was Dolores and not Doris, and if she posed for Jacob Epstein, then she was probably Dolores, the famous artists' model who was born Norine Fournier Schofield and was married to Frank Amsden, Harry Sadler, and George Lattimore. She apparently did not marry a man named Carlyle. Dolores published her memoirs, written with the assistance of Maud Ffoulkes, as "By Dolores, 'The Fatal Woman' of the London Studios," which appeared in *The American Weekly*, the Sunday supplement to the Hearst newspapers, in 1930: 26 January, pp. 12–13, 22; 2 February, pp. 14–15, 20; 9 February, pp. 12–13, 24; 16 February, pp. 10–11, 20; 23 February, pp. 12–13, 24; 2 March, pp. 14–15; 9 March, pp. 14–15; 16 March, pp. 14–15, 25; 23 March, pp. 12–13, 24; 30 March, pp. 12–13, 22. (References are to *The American Weekly* that accompanied the *San Francisco Examiner*.) Dolores was not known as the Queen of Greenwich Village—she apparently never visited the United States—although she refers to herself as Queen of the Bohemia in her "Dolores, Famous Artists' Model, in a Dime Museum," *The American Weekly*, 6 August 1933, p. 12. Another Dolores became famous as a dancer with the Ziegfeld Follies, beginning in 1917. In 1923 she moved to Paris and married the wealthy William Tudor Wilkinson. She was born Kathleen Rose in London. A woman named Vivian Denton claimed to be the model Dolores's daughter, but her case was unconvincing because she confused the two Doloreses (see "She Put the 2 Doloreses Together and Spelled M-O-T-H-E-R," *New York Daily Mirror* Magazine Section, 16 September 1934, pp. 3, 19). Bald also seems to be combining the two Doloreses into one person.

Tuesday, 4 November 1930, p. 4.

Ezra Pound has been engaged as associate editor of *The New Review*, the Montparnasse monthly whose first number will appear on January 1, 1931.

Shoulder to shoulder, Samuel Putnam, its editor and publisher, and the jovial Voice from Rapallo, will march toward an "honesty" in literature. Together, they will fight the "corpse-raisers, pretenders and cheap miracle men of the past decade."

The cafés are filled with it; writers are cursing it; people are talking about it. Something is going to happen. Last Tuesday, the entire Quarter was placarded with copies of "Direction," which sweetly damned the whole gang of Joyce-leaning "experimenters," hitherto quite secure.[1]

Putnam was behind that, and his war cry may be summed up: "There is an end even to experiments and we feel that the end has been reached in the year 1930." And then we catch the shibboleths: "False modernism," and "Attitudes become platitudes." We learn that James Joyce is about as modern as Rabelais and that he "merely has wed native Irish blarney to the late medieval *fatrasie*." In short, Putnam contends that the so-called moderns are fumblers in the fascinating but obscure and exhausted realm of the subconscious. He will fight for a "concisive and incisive intelligence." And he got Ezra Pound to help him.

This is serious. If Putnam has his way, the smart "stream of consciousness" will change neither its direction nor its dimensions. The stream will utterly freeze and on its surface will skate the tall, ascetic Samuel Putnam followed by his long line of converts; while on the sidelines the irrepressible Ezra Pound will wave and cheer until the year 1941, when the next manifesto will give us more ideas.

America is recovering from the measles, as exemplified by the New Humanism; which is not fatal, according to Putnam, if succeeded by an American art and not a "badly garbled European carry-over."

The New Review will make much of dawning America. It follows then that the publication will run rather heavily to the very modern arts. What are they? Phonographs, talkies, jazz, folding beds, plumbing. For illustrations, photographs should be used. This department recommends a full-page snapshot called *Interior* or *What Every Home Must Have*. It will help interpret the American art spirit and might tickle interior decorators with a new ideology for an old compulsion.

* * *

1. The placard "Direction," written by Samuel Putnam, Harold Salemson, and Richard Thoma, encourages emphasizing literary content, not form. No copy is known to exist. See Putnam, *Paris Was Our Mistress* (New York: Viking, 1947), pp. 226–29.

Tuesday, 11 November 1930, p. 4.

In my solid moments, I sometimes consider this cold age. Has caution killed romance? Has the picaresque aroma entirely disappeared? Is the world turning flat? Not that it really matters, but sometimes our period worries me.

Whenever upset that way, my thoughts turn to the Contessa Monici. When I think of her, I bubble with relief, for she holds Montparnasse in the palm of her plump, white hand. She is the spirit behind the throne. What's more, she's genuine and that's rare.

From infancy, the Contessa Monici has lived at a blind gallop. Sometimes her impulses have been slapped by society, which only changed their direction. Among other places, she has lived in a convent, a jail and a mad house. Now she lives in the Parc Montsouris. To me, she is the arch-Bohemian of Montparnasse.

Inhibitions? She waves them off with dynamite. If they ever came too close, she would frighten them out of the psychology books. She says she was *très* curious at the age of five. The accompanying photograph entitled *The Curve of Art* reveals the Contessa Monici tempting Raymond Duncan with a paint brush. Careful perusal shows sensitive Raymond poised for laughter.

Incidentally, the Contessa is a good painter and she makes a portrait in one hour. "In one *pouf*," as she expresses it. But that's away off the subject. It is difficult to describe her psychic massages because the very contemplation of her complexities makes me dizzy. She is never dull. Every nerve of her screams with exuberance. I have seen her shout, sing, weep and begin a portrait before I half-finished a cigarette. At a formal party, at her Montsouris apartment, I have watched her trip into the room dressed as you see her on this page. And then begin to sing. Remember that once she was prima donna with the Scala Opera Company of Milan, and that she had been a star pupil of Puccini. And that she sang opposite Charles Hackett of the Metropolitan Opera Company. Why shouldn't her guests have fun?

On the other hand, she can look like a school teacher on the terrace of the Dôme. Her values are her own and she knows them, but she has paid for her temperament. Her memoirs, almost completed, are being scrambled for by the publishers.[1] Her life has been a perpendicular pendulum, but I think she knows more of hell. Her wild escapades may be frowned upon, but their narration should contribute to the relief of the whimpering beast in everyone.

Not long ago, England kicked her out as an undesirable alien. She returned in male attire, was arrested and put in jail. Since then, she has been known as "The Smuggled Countess."

Once one of her admirers tried to get rid of her by having her confined in a nut house. Her experience there would shock a newspaperman.

Last February (the 12th to be exact) she married Captain Paterson. The affair was headline stuff. Among the guests were Gilbert White, Derain, Foujita, Domergue, Zadkine, Kisling, Beltràn y Masses and 50 others. Imagine the embarrassment of the groom and the bride when they realized they couldn't pay the dinner bill. They burned the wires, sold two paintings, and the revels went on.

The Contessa had hobnobbed with Mussolini and Marinetti. Her stories about both are very funny. Her closest friend was Isadora Duncan. The adventures of these two are legends in Montparnasse. She preferred Isadora's personality to the dynamics and "nodules" of men like Marinetti. Dukes and princes have fought duels over her in romantic Italy, but she never took them or their duels seriously. She has hobnobbed with gamblers who rub vaseline on their fingers. One of them once set her up as a stake.

Oscar Wilde came to her after his dark adventure. He started to write *Mrs. Daventry*, because he was inspired by the color of her hair.[2] She spent three months making an opalescent goblet for Oscar. When it got to him, he was dead. I wish I could tell a few stories about the Contessa and Oscar. They are very funny. This could go on, but it's getting late. You may see the arch-Bohemian around the Dôme, or you may be invited to one of her cocktail parties. All I can say is that knowing her is like a spasm.

*

1. Contessa Lina Monici apparently did not publish her memoirs.
2. After beginning *Mr. and Mrs. Daventry*, probably in 1897, Oscar Wilde sold the scenario to several parties, including Frank Harris, who finished writing the play.

Tuesday, 23 December 1930, p. 4.

The first number of *The New Review*, published in Montparnasse, will appear in a couple of weeks. Highbrows and lowbrows will sing in the same chorus.

Talk in the cafés reveals a definite curiosity about Putnam's magazine.

Already it has been learned that Maxwell Bodenheim will flash on aesthetics and life, and that Jean Cocteau contributes "Angel Wuthercut." Confucius will be criticized.

But the editor does not despise the *Rhapsody in Blue*. It has been learned that there will be notes on jazz, and even the radio will be given a chance.

It is evident, then, that *The New Review* is the organ of no school or movement. If it has a trend, the direction may become manifest as the successive numbers appear. In the second number, for instance, Mussolini contributes a long revelatory confession, while V. F. Calverton throws the bent looking-glass on lucky Sinclair Lewis. Above all, Ezra Pound is one of the associate editors.

The cards up Putnam's sleeve are puzzling Montparnasse. This unsentimental publicist, who is as familiar with the shapes and smells of erudition as is a milkmaid with all the barnyard secrets, insists that lusty Americana [*sic*] will always nourish the dream. The modern American spirit is an indispensable gland.

Putnam's recent American version of Rabelais pushed his name over the literary gardens, and since then he has been freely condemned but always respected. He is cold, but magnetic. Last week he signed a contract with Richard Smith to write a book on the life of John Calvin. Pirandello, recently seen here, has asked Putnam to translate twelve of his short stories.

Putnam's *European Caravan* has just been completed.[1] His magazine, *The New Review*, may start new caravans trailing towards new mysteries. The circle is growing.

*
*　*

1. See p. 21, n. 8, and p. 33, n. 1. Samuel Putnam evidently did not write a book on John Calvin. He translated four volumes by Luigi Pirandello: *As You Desire Me* (New York: Dutton, 1931); *Horse in the Moon* (New York: Dutton, 1932); *Tonight We Improvise* (New York: Dutton, 1932); *One, None and a Hundred-Thousand* (New York: Dutton, 1933).

Tuesday, 30 December 1930, p. 4.

On Christmas Eve, a man with long yellow hair broke from the crowd and rushed to the middle of the street. In one hand, there was a violin; in the other, a bow. In the center of the taxi melee, he played a rhapsody and then directed traffic with his bow before the cops could get to him. The mob on the sidewalks cheered. Christmas Eve in Montparnasse.

The same evening, I saw the Countess at Jimmie's bar. She was writing something.

"What are you writing?" I asked.

"A novel about Christmas," she said, finishing a beer.

The gang at the bar laughed. Jimmie was roaring behind the bar.

"What's it about?" I asked.

The Countess sighed.

"Santa Claus," she bellowed. Her voice was husky. She began reading from the first page of her manuscript: "Santa Claus is not a myth, but he is in one way. What about the girls who wait for Santa Claus day after day, year after year, and the years to come?"

"How do you like that for a start?" asked the Countess. I told her.

"Jingle Bells," said the Countess. "This book will be written in barrels of tears. Now, heart to heart and mind to mind, don't you think it's a good beginning?" Her eyes were as round as candle ends and as clear as bubbles. "Answer," she said. I did and she sighed gratefully. Christmas Eve in Montparnasse.

I ran as fast as I could to the ruggery of Raymond Duncan. The patient weaver was cleaning with benzine some egg stains from the train of his skirt.

"Will the condition of the Stock Market affect Christmas in Montparnasse?" I asked.

Raymond raised his eyes. He said: "I place my hand on my heart—strange! It beats not to the cry of quotations, but in rhythm with the fresh air of the sky, which enters through my nostrils and goes out through my mouth."

"Talk to me," I said, "about the sidewalks of Montparnasse."

Raymond said: "I'll talk about universal sidewalks. They should be covered with carpets and not jar people's feet.

"This inspiration has come to me first rather than to another because my bare feet, more sensitive than high heels and silk stockings, are capable of judging pavements."

Christmas in Montparnasse.

There is a luxury in wandering and wondering, and Gwen Le Gallienne loves that luxury. She writes from the wilds of Corsica: "Farewell to the worldly world for a long while. Now I am free from the tearing and pulling of masculine civilization. At times I am almost happy."

Gwen travels with paints, easels, and an extra pair of khaki pants on her back. At present she is staying with a popular Russian woman, Mariska Dietrich. Later she will hike to Tunis, Spain and Egypt.

She writes, "Now that there is air and space, I see and hear clearly."

Quelle différence! Two months ago, I sat with Gwen at the Select. Her voice was limp and her interesting mouth drooped helplessly. She sat there rigid and annoyed.

"Sometimes," she said, "I am so bored that I haven't the energy to cross the street. Have you ever tasted lethargy?"

I said that I never had.

"Then," she said, "you don't know. Insipidity is worse than cruelty. Reality is insipidity; if only I could scratch long furrows in the moon." She closed her eyes. "I love my art but I live for the dream. My dear, you must have heard of kinetic romance. I must be suffering from it."

That was two months ago. Now Gwen's inner life is being nourished by travel.

The letter concludes with: "I have been meeting all kinds of déclassé nobles and aristocrats of all countries."

These sports will never know Gwen or her empyreal wants. They never will understand that her tapestry is interwoven with clouds spun from vague memories sterilized in a Grecian urn. Hold it!

When resting, Gwen paints. The conclusion of her present pilgrimage will be celebrated by a joint exhibit in Paris and New York. Now she garners rich images as she climbs and tramps with her pet cat, Chang of Siam. And it is understood in Montparnasse that Gwen has other plans.

The galloping Le Gallienne wants to start a girls' college for the benefit of young sublimators anxious for instruction in the more plastic arts.

The layers of Gwen's soul have their own understanding, for she feels her own comprehensibility. The image is the thing, and Gwen ascends the moon beams. This "kinetic" romantic regards desire as an orange and beauty as a grove. Her life and her art are her own, and no new movement is beyond her native wisdom.

*

Tuesday, 6 January 1931, p. 4.

*
* *

Everyone is going south. Last Friday night, I watched the ever-colorful Laurence Vail dismantle his studio in the Avenue du Maine. Vail is considered colorful because he looks like a Viking, wears salmon-shaded shirts and paints surrealistic pictures. In addition to that, he writes catching prose. He talks jerkily, smiles naively and thinks deeply. He, too, was going south. Apparently, every significant person, not paralyzed by inertia or a job, has deserted the Dôme.

While watching Vail pack, I picked up one of his old manuscripts—"A Great One"—and was caught by the prose. It was a bitter satire, a paragraph of which follows:

Is this the end? How can there ever be an end to the universe ruled by friction? Thing will continue to rub thing, thus making fret—the foot that kicks the whining dog, the sulky sweetheart, bright tin cans and jolly footballs. If you disbelieve me, rub the panorama with your eyeball. Walking, even standing still, you rub the ground; dead, you rub boards that exert pressure on the earth; thus, alive or dead, you make holes or dents in stuff around—air, woman, water, dirt, which elements, pressed back, rub one another, fret, sprout weeds, children, constellations. Lassitude spat a mirage. . . . This thought and others occupied my mind one autumnal evening in a city that smelt like London.

I was agreeably startled by Vail's announcement that his book, *Murder! Murder!* has at last found a publisher. It is a horror story caked with humor; and to cap it all, the poet Alfred Kreymborg has written an introduction.[1]

Vail's surrealistic drawings were piled neatly in a large box. One group is called the *Nightmare Series*. It represents earthworms, shooting stars, waltzing fish and tropical plants imbued with human features. These features were affixed with colored hat pins and wads of chewing gum—hat pins for the eyes and gum for the mouths. There is a story in Montparnasse that Vail was once so frightened by one of his own drawings that he ran in terror from his studio. I asked him about that. He said that he didn't run but admitted after close questioning that he walked out with great celerity. All of which proves that if art does not grip the layman, it generally grips the artist.

The next day (Saturday) Vail left for Villefranche, where he has purchased a chateau. I understand that a number of important people will have the keys of the house. Among them are Kay Boyle, Link Gillespie, Lady Mary Reynolds, the gardener, Alfred Kreymborg, Dorothy Kreymborg, Eugene Jolas, Nina Wilcox Putnam, and Marcel Duchamp. The last named is regarded in Montparnasse as the famous one-picture man. They tell me that he once painted *Nude Descending a Staircase* (about 1913) and hasn't bothered since.[2]

That will be an interesting colony. Kreymborg is a good chess player. He can beat Vail, but Vail was beaten by Sindbad, his eight-year-old son. Kreymborg is reported to have beaten Capablanca, but I doubt it, because Sindbad, the infant, beat Kreymborg, the poet. Kreymborg insists that he spotted Sindbad a bishop and wasn't concentrating anyway. It's a terrible mixup.

*

1. Laurence Vail, "A Great One," *transition*, 14 (Fall 1928), pp. 151–63. The quotation is from p. 159. See p. 13, n. 1. Vail's novel has no Kreymborg introduction.
2. Marcel Duchamp painted *Nude Descending a Staircase* in 1912 and exhibited it at the New York Armory Show in 1913.

Tuesday, 13 January 1931, p. 4.

Princess Désirée gave a *soirée* at her Montparnasse chateau last Friday night. About 30 boys and girls huddled about the lamps and candles while bottles of rum disappeared into the shadows. It was an informal occasion.

Interest was supplied by Helba Huara, a half-blood Indian from Peru. Her dance numbers were significant and coercive. Recently she was featured at the Guild Theatre and Schubert's in New York. You will observe that the two photographs nicknamed *Savage* and *Soul too* explain in a measure the charm of Bohemia. They represent the two polarities; and the intermediate nuances between which human beings flit, were interpreted by the dancing Inca. That girl took Broadway by its tall buildings and didn't let go until she decided to come to Paris.

Before she went into her numbers, the crowd was a bit restive. This, despite the fact that the Princess, a Russian, speaks English with a Scotch accent and is thoroughly conversant with German. Lajos Tihanyi, the Hungarian painter, now exhibiting at the Editions Bonaparte, acted as usher. He was assisted by Gyula Halász, a Hungarian journalist. Director Franck of the Comédie Française was one of the guests. Then there was Pierre Corodische, a movie director.

Mary Coles was late. Kathlyn Parker, the actress,[1] was surrounded by Toni Gross, Hungarian; Bill Hayter, English; Philip Evergood, American; and Magnus Hening, German. I also saw Della Husband, the Canadian painter, just back from Canada.

Helba's dancing may be described as startling. As she went through her performance, the candles on the floor fluttered weakly. When she concluded the one called *Savage*, which delicately illustrated the benefit of a supreme moment, several of the men and two of the girls were on the border of hysterics. In fact, those who were sitting got up on their feet, while those who were standing, sat down. But I remained calm.

The room was all done up in green (El Greco effect) which in a measure accounted for the macabre note, but there was something in the manner in which Helba manipulated the castanets and tapped her heels that cannot be explained. The broken rhythms of the castanet tom-tom communicated strange meanings to the artists and writers. Indeed there was nothing flower-like about the motifs. On the contrary, they were sinister, revolutionary. Her movements were as fluent as the prose poems of Gerturde Stein.

1. Bald possibly refers to the actress Catherine Parker.

Tuesday, 27 January 1931, p. 4.

Talk on literary tendencies has been stimulated by the appearance of the maiden number of *The New Review*, published in Montparnasse.

On the cover, I see the familiar names of Maxwell Bodenheim, Ezra

Pound and Jean Cocteau. Of Montparnasse talent, there are contributions by Horace Bevans, Richard Thoma, Willard Widney and George Reavey.[1]

The policy of *The New Review* appears to be a clean, masculine clarification of the air, which is still heavy with the fumes of the late Garbage Era. By clean, I mean incisive and objective, with all the hysteria trimmed off. Indeed, there was something of the same coin between "Myths, myths, give us more myths" and the ageless "Button, button, who's got the button." I hope *The New Review* never sinks into that.

The most definite statement of the allied aim comes from Massimo Bontempelli, head of the Italian division. The founder of the Italian Novecento contributes "900," wherein he states:

> It is not so much for enchantments as for adventure that we are athirst; we thirst after life viewed as a miraculous adventure, as a perpetual risk. . . . To be always upon a tight-rope or upon the top of a wave—and still to smile and light one's pipe. . . . Creation is to be considered as an isolated expression, perfect in itself, free of precedents or of consequences.[2]

The Spanish contributor, Giménez Caballero, informs us that "Advance guardism as a genetic force may be looked upon as dead and done for." He points to the split of the "isms" and to the fact that Marinetti, the father of Futurism, is now the docile father of children.[3]

It is not surprising, then, that *The New Review* is attracted to the modern arts, such as photography, the cinema and radio. They are regarded as the means and end of construction. We read of the "photography of music," "radio opera," and the goals of the tonal film.

George Antheil writes: "The radio and gramophone are the musical tabloids of today. They will not be interesting until a Man Ray of musical photography does something utterly different with them. . . . The tone-film is the music of tomorrow. New musical worlds rest undiscovered, etc."[4]

This concern with the art possibilities of mechanics appears to be the first law of the new constitution. Bontempelli is the most merciless ogre to the younger writers. "Let us hope," he says, "that the cinema, which is so magnificently taking the place of the theatre as well as of the novel, will succeed in starving men of letters to the point where they will be obliged to choose some other trade."[5]

The attainment of culture, that popular daisy field for butterflies and cuff-shooting scholars, is being ruled out. Today acquaintanceship with thousands of books (including "good" literature) has become so common that only fools brag about it. In fact, many try to live it down but, unfortunately, it is often too late. Few of the addicts ever take one step backward to measure its relationship to their own personal significance. That's a hard one. As for "culture," let me blushingly add that, although aware of its penalties, I can turn a factory girl into a cultured woman in six months.

The lusty Ezra Pound, in an editorial proclamation entitled "After Election," tells what he thinks on several planes from Joyce to journalists.[6]

Jean Cocteau contributes "Angel Wuthercut." Here are a few lines:

> Out with your sword,
> Come in slow motion mad star.
> Why have I not your body? Oh!
> If we but had your hips
> Stone-draped, mean
> Ladybug a-bounding. . . .
> Angel Wuthercut, with the animal feet
> Sky-blue, has come. I am alone. . . .[7]

These lines give a glimpse of the idea and purpose of Cocteau's film *Life of a Poet*. "Angel Wuthercut" promises to be the most discussed poem of today. It is understood that Cocteau wrote that during an opium jag.

Maxwell Bodenheim's essay, "Esthetics, Criticism and Life," has the usual exceptional Bodenheim quality. I have always respected his poetry and enjoyed two of his novels, and readily declare that the essay looks imposing. Anything abstruse looks imposing. But the essay in question is a sorry exhibition. The poet dives into metaphysics and comes up gasping for nine pages. His thesis would be considered elementary stuff by any college student of philosophy: "The disorder of esthetics is incalculable, infinite. Any invasion by science or pure reason is futile, is as pathetic as the buzzing of a

50

wingless fly in a bottle. The invasion is futile because the bottle is bigger than the fly."[8] That was the argument. One can read that stuff in a much nicer style in the lucid pages of Santayana or a hundred other books on the subject.

On the other hand, his sentence power is arresting. Although they lack the author's customary splenetic vigor, they are sonorous and deceptive. But I don't see their place in any new review. It is with relief, then, that I learn that Liveright has just brought out *Naked on Roller Skates*, by Maxwell Bodenheim. That's more in his line.[9]

*

1. *New Review*, 1.1 (January-February 1931), includes Maxwell Bodenheim's "Esthetics, Criticism, and Life," pp. 1–9, and "The Inner Hermit" (a review of Margaret Anderson's *My Thirty Years' War*), pp. 63–65; Ezra Pound's "After Election," pp. 53–55; Jean Cocteau's "Angel Wuthercut," pp. 10–14; Horace Bevans's "Document and the Dream: The Breviary of the Drug" (a review of Jean Cocteau's *Opium*), pp. 65–66, and "Book Notes," pp. 67–68; Richard Thoma's "Last Poem," p. 45, and "Cinema: First Filming of a Poem; Silent Talking Picture" (a review of Cocteau's *The Life of a Poet*, which was later entitled *Le Sang d'un poete* [*The Blood of a Poet*]), pp. 57–59; Willard Widney's "Records: Notes on New Jazz," pp. 60–61; and George Reavey's "A Survey of Russian Literature Since the Revolution," pp. 27–37. Bald's "From Work in Static" appears on pp. 55–57.
2. Massimo Bontempelli, " '900,' " *New Review*, pp. 15–20. The quotation is from pp. 16–17.
3. E. Giménez Caballero, "1918 Spanish Literature 1930," *New Review*, pp. 20–26. The quotation is from p. 21.
4. George Antheil, "Musical Theatre," *New Review*, pp. 59–60. The quotation is from p. 59.
5. Bontempelli, p. 20.
6. Pound, pp. 53–55.
7. Cocteau, p. 11.
8. This quotation is not from Bodenheim's "Esthetics, Criticism, and Life."
9. Bodenheim, *Naked on Roller Skates* (New York: Liveright, 1931).

Tuesday, 17 February 1931, p. 4.

They are waving flags in Montparnasse. They are beating their drums again. Jimmie is going to be married.

Seven months ago, Jimmie whispered in my ear: "Romance is romance, isn't it? Love is love, isn't it?"

Before replying, I studied him for half an hour. Then I said: "Always." I was flattered by his confidence.

Love is like a trapeze. Jimmie sprang for it and is now swinging into matrimony. It happened in Deauville last summer. She is French.

Jimmie smiles bashfully as his friends shake his hands. But he is not afraid, even after he was warned that on wedding nights tragedy is born. May there be new patterns ever![1]

Last week, I said: "What are you doing to prepare yourself?"

He replied: "I am keeping in perfect shape. Every day, I skip the rope, do shadow boxing and take long runs through the Bois de Boulogne." The accompanying photo shows Jimmie in a training moment.

Jimmie is the hero of half a dozen novels. Caricatures of him in all poses and moods have been circulated in a hundred papers of America. Photographs of this figure decorate the walls of numerous popular bars on both sides of the Seine. Novelists have dubbed him the most "natural" barman in Paris. He is probably the most popular individual in Montparnasse. Why? I don't know. I only call your attention to the weekly load of mail that reaches him from every corner of the States. They keep writing to him after they go back.

A long time ago Jimmie was an actor, as was his father before him. Then he became a prize fighter. From the *Epicurean*, a popular Paris guide, I learn that in his day he "fought them all at his weight."[2] He still does.

A couple of weeks ago, five cab drivers were boisterous in a small all-night bar. They annoyed a small party that Jimmie knew. He vaulted over a couple of chairs, aimed in several directions, and three sat down on the floor. The others walked off.

In a rash moment, I was lured to the local gym where he trains. We put on eight-ounce gloves after he promised to be lenient. I hit the air a dozen times and then, exasperated, I timed a beautiful one from the floor, and let it fly. It struck nothing with such power that a tendon of my right hip was strained. They took me home in a taxi, and for the rest of that week the injured tendon was massaged regularly by my concierge.

Until recently, Jimmie was found at the Falstaff. Now he runs his own bar across the street with Frère Eddie, formerly of Ciro's.[3] They attract the literati; they attract the artists. Soon there will be an additional attraction. And so it goes. And so it goes. Life is like that.

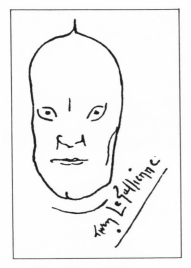

Aleister Crowley by Gwen Le
Gallienne

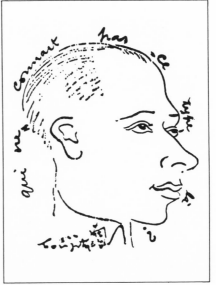

Henri Broca by Foujita

Gwen Le Gallienne by Gwen Le Gallienne

The Dôme

"At the Dôme" by Nina Hamnett

From the left: Laurence Vail, Kay Boyle, Alfred Kreymborg, Clotilde Vail, and Dorothy Kreymborg, 1930s
From the Kay Boyle Collection, Special Collections, Morris Library, Southern Illinois University at Carbondale

Kiki by Hilaire Hiler
Courtesy, Hilaire Hiler, Jr.

Flossie Martin by Hilaire Hiler
Courtesy, Hilaire Hiler, Jr.

Jimmie Charters by Hilaire Hiler
Courtesy, Hilaire Hiler, Jr.

Foujita by Hilaire Hiler
Courtesy, Hilaire Hiler, Jr.

June Mansfield (Miller)
Courtesy, Tony, Valentine, and Barbara Miller

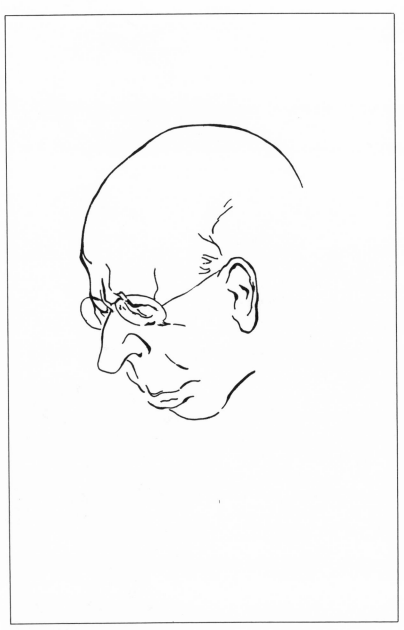

Henry Miller by Abraham Rattner
From *The Happy Rock: A Book About Henry Miller*, publisher/editor Bern Porter

Abraham Lincoln Gillespie, Jr.

George Seldes, France, 1929
Courtesy, George Seldes

William Seabrook and Marjorie Worthington at Colomb Bechar
Courtesy, Mrs. William Seabrook

*
* *

1. Jimmie did not marry the woman, whose name was Madeleine. See James Charters, *This Must Be the Place* (London: Joseph, 1934), pp. 280–84; (New York: Furman, 1937), pp. 300–304.
2. Source unknown.
3. Jimmie left the Falstaff for the Bec de Gaz. His partner was Eddie Ruffi. See *This Must Be the Place*, p. 216 (English edition), p. 289 (American edition).

Tuesday, 10 March 1931, p. 4.

Cagnes is trembling. An earthquake has hit Cagnes. There is a new movement in art down there.

All of that is none of my business except that the boys in the south are children of Montparnasse. Indeed, Montparnasse is a fertile woman with a big capacity for love—but a bigger one for appreciation. Some of her lovers are just sons of badinage, but the legitimate ones are always of interest.

Hilaire Hiler, one of the best boys in the family, is launching a discovery that has them shouting, and Ezra Pound is in a passion. Ezra has been following Hiler's work for years, and when he saw his latest, declared: "Lock up your studio or the wolves will steal it!" Ezra wanted him to wait until due acknowledgment was awarded. It is a fact that although creation is born in purity, the mawlers are right behind.

But the news is out. The latest paintings are on exhibit at the Allan Gallery, Cannes. The movement is called Neonaturism. In this article, we can give only a crude idea of what it is all about. Hiler, who has been appointed art editor of *The New Review*, will present a detailed explanation with sketches in *The New Review*'s next number. George Antheil, a leading advocate, will also contribute a summary of Neonaturism.

The new movement stresses what may be termed the new reality, a tendency prevailing throughout Europe in different *métiers*, and some of the proponents see a parallel in the *Neue Sachlichkeit* now popular in Germany. The American product is based on the principle that the object should be approached through abstraction without losing itself in the latter's vagaries. Instead of floating in a dream, arbitrarily designed, this "ism" accepts reality but retains the working principles of modern art.

The new art insists on geometric precision, basing this thesis, in part, on our modern machine-eye. Accordingly a slight deflection from a right angle causes great suffering.

Which gives us geometry appeal. Will this obviate sex appeal? Not entirely because trees can't fly.

I know that Hiler employs an infinite variety of instruments for the sake of precision. His stock of brushes has long been the talk of the Quarter. He uses sable brushes, hair brushes, camel brushes, lynx brushes and some nicely shingled.

Succeeding the Futurism of Italy, Surrealism of France and Rayonism of Germany, we now have Neonaturism, an American product. Those of us who have known Hiler for years and studied his experiments and their development were of the opinion that if an American here or back home should succeed in evolving a new working principle in art, money bet on Hiler was pretty safe money. Citizens returning from the south are noisy in their acclamations. You may judge for yourself after reading his article or seeing his exhibit in Paris which should take place next fall.

Some people remember Hiler as a writer, some as a scientist, some as the quondam owner of the Jockey. The latter was years ago, and it gives a gentle twinge to the veterans who pass the exterior of the Jockey. The somewhat extravagant but appropriate figures painted on that wall were committed by him about six years ago during a gay hour. The literary know him through his articles on art and especially on his book, *From Nudity to Raiment*.[1] In his early days he was also a musician. These statistics are recited to prove that versatility can prove anything. But now, he wishes to be known only as an artist. He is even art's latest father. Watch the family spread.

1. Hilaire Hiler, *From Nudity to Raiment* (New York: Weyhe, 1929; London: Foyle, 1929; London: Marshall, 1929; Paris: Librairie de France; New York: Weyhe, 1929).

Tuesday, 17 March 1931, p. 4.

Two of my secret service men, who have been shadowing Gwen Le Gallienne for the past three weeks, report that she is not in jail. Gwen was arrested as a bandit.

On the outskirts of Menton, a bandit was being hunted by the police. They rounded up everyone they could find, and in their haste pinched Gwen.

It was no one's fault. Gwen, who will be romantic, was hiking about the country in her famous blue velvet pants.

"Imagine!" says the report. "The police were dumbfounded when they discovered that she was neither a boy nor a bandit. She was only a painter."

Gwen wrote a long letter explaining the situation. "Everyone else is stupidly wearing pajamas, but I will wear what I please. The police were very nice to me."

It must be remembered that Gwen was born and reared a romantic. In the wilds of Connecticut, she had known tree tops, lumber camps, house boats and Elbert Hubbard. She loves Montparnasse, but she gets bored, "just bored to tears." The layers of her loneliness are puzzling. She spends most of her time now hiking—always hiking. Gwen hikes up and down the Riviera.

The report discloses that recently Gwen was playing the wheels of Monte Carlo. There she met all sorts of people, some of whom were interesting and some déclassé. "It is better to be bored in numbers," Gwen once remarked.

The photo entitled *Nonchalance* shows Gwen with a friend. Our heroine is the taller one with Gray River, the dog. How could the police have been so stupid?

Gwen said, "In all the world, there is painting and genius . . . but there is also rubbish and bad smells. The world is the home of petty jealousies. Sometimes I feel drawn and quartered."

I wrote Gwen a hysterical entreaty begging her to return at once to Montparnasse where beauty and poetry will always triumph . . . where progress is not too expansive and culture not over-fastidious . . . where she may express herself prodigiously.

*

Tuesday, 31 March 1931, p. 4.

The New Review is a magazine published in Montparnasse without benefit of clergy. The next number will appear very shortly and we shall review it on this page.

Samuel Putnam, editor of *The New Review,* leaves for a lecture tour in America in a couple of weeks. He has been commissioned to give a series of talks in connection with *The European Caravan* which he edited and his biography of Marguerite of Navarre.

Putnam has just finished translating 12 short stories by Pirandello. The volume will probably be called *Horse in the Moon*. (The recent sweepstakes may have had something to do with that title.) Pirandello is also responsible for *As You Desire Me*, a play running at the Elliot Theatre, of which Putnam is making a literary adaptation.[1]

This Putnam is a busy man. In conjunction with Richard Thoma, one of the associate editors of *The New Review*, he is working on the libretto for George Antheil's next opera, based on *Les Enfants Terribles*, translated last year by the same phenomenon.[2]

Then he sends a weekly letter to the New York *Sun*, wherein he describes the Paris literary fashions.[3] Incidentally, the Gotham Book Mart of New York will be the American distributors of *The New Review*.

Six feet two he stands, a silent—oh hell, we have a photograph of him which we promised not to use. But we will. Sure we will.

George Seldes writes from America that he hopes to be married without further delay. George recently wrote an article on Mussolini for *Scribner's*. Is there a connection? He also wrote a big book with the word "terror" in the title.[4]

* * *

Isadora Duncan had the spirit, if not the brains, of Plato. (Let's not quarrel about that.) The language of the dance had provided a tentative form easily rationalized but the form supplied little more than a glimpse of that spirit. Nor did the penny biographers bring us closer to Isadora after she was gone.

An old Parnassian offers a commemorative exposition of Isadora Duncan at the Galerie E. Brummer—the vernissage tomorrow. For an appreciable period, Abraham Walkowitz followed the dancer through the mazes of her emotional life, until he could anticipate her gestures, her confidences, her hysterias. The two were cronies when Isadora occupied an apartment now painted red by a giant vertical sign of a jazz palace in the Rue Delambre.

In those days Isadora, Bob Chanler, Aleister Crowley and Walkowitz used to snap their fingers in unison. That was music. At the exhibit commencing tomorrow, Walkowitz will show crayon sketches, watercolors and paintings, which should bring back to most of us an ancient epoch.

Kiki is the Queen of Montparnasse. She was elected by her friends a few years ago at a blowout at the Bobino. Kiki has been a model, café singer and movie actress. You may hear her sing any night at the Oceanic Bar in the Edgar Quinet district.

Broca was one of the cleverest caricaturists in the Quarter. He comes from that region of France commonly referred to as *Midi moins le quart*, which may have accounted for the volubility of his speech. Broca was brilliant.

Kiki is still popular after her fashion, despite the usual battle with heft. She still is the life of the party. For many years the two were excellent friends.

Neither of them has missed anything, but Kiki had less imagination and more vitality. Kiki is still Kiki, but Broca has collapsed and is obliged to rest in a local sanatorium.

*

1. See p. 33, n. 1, and p. 43, n. 1. Samuel Putnam, *Marguerite of Navarre* (New York: Coward-McCann, 1935; London: Jarrolds, 1936).
2. George Antheil did not base an opera on *Les Enfants terribles*. See p. 21, n. 8.
3. The *New York Sun* began publishing Samuel Putnam's letters in 1929.
4. George Seldes, "Twilight of the Dictators," *Scribner's*, 89.5 (May 1931), pp. 465–76. See p. 28, n. 3.

Tuesday, 7 April 1931, p. 4.

Ezra Pound comes to town next Thursday. The strong man of Rapallo will go into a huddle with Samuel Putnam, editor of *The New Review*. The next number will be out in eight days. Feathers will fly.

George Reavey, one of our Irish poets, is editing the English edition of *Formes*. He is also writing a series of *Faust* poems.[1] Reavey is Cambridge, mild and quiet. Let us call attention to his red chin weeds. They cover a good story. Caught in the Russian Revolution, the poet was tapped on the chin with a brick, which left a tiny scar. The beard covers it.

Another Irish poet now among us is Samuel Beckett, instructor at the University of Dublin. His book on Proust has just been published in London.[2]

One more Irish poet who is rising fast is Thomas McGreevy, whose book on Eliot, previously reviewed in the *Tribune*, is causing a stir.[3] We understand that 600 copies were sold in London the first day. He is living in Florence at the moment.

*
* *

We drank tea with Gertrude Stein a few days ago. She lives quietly with another woman in the Rue de Fleurus, about ten jumps from the Dôme. For the past 25 years, Gertrude has been saving the English language from that studio.

The walls are covered with Picasso. One of them is a portrait of Gertrude herself, for which she sat 91 times. That portrait and the actual Gertrude immediately put the visitor in his place. But John, who was with me, said: "Your prose, I think, is obscure."

"My prose," said she who looks like Caesar, "is obscure only to the lazy-minded. It is like a deep well."

"Some people," said John, "are inclined to believe that it is a bottomless well or one with a false bottom."

John was a bit cruel. After all, Gertrude had been a star pupil of William James. She had graduated with high honors from Johns Hopkins. She has mastered the run of the sciences and her knowledge of literature is oceanic.

"I'll give you," said the writer, "a lesson in American history." Her eye is clear and her voice is incisive. Gertrude does not stutter when she talks. Here is what she said:

> America made the 20th century just as England made the 19th. We have given Europe everything.
>
> The natural line of descent is the big four: Poe to Whitman to James to myself. I am the last.

"You are the last?" said John.

"Of course. My reputation is international and is spreading all the time."

"There is James Joyce," said John.

Gertrude smiled.

"You would, of course. Joyce is *good*. He is a *good* writer. Let's not say anything about that. But who started the whole thing? My first great book, *The Making of Americans*, was published in 1905.[4] That was long before the birth of *Ulysses*. But Joyce has done something even if his influence is local. John Synge, another Irish writer, has had his day. Have some more tea."

This fellow John is implacable. He followed with: "I understand that Wyndham Lewis drops you into the Anita Loos category. The naive approach. . . ."⁵

"Wyndham wrote that, of course. But all that is British propaganda against great American writers." John almost dropped his spoon. Gertrude went on: "You might learn that American writing is signalized by the consistent tendency towards abstraction without mysticism. There is no mysticism in my work."

John had nothing more to say. We went back to the Dôme.

Those who are interested in Austrian literature might like to read the current number of *This Quarter*, published here. The names are good and representative, although we did miss the favorite Wedekind and Karl Kraus. The latter, who for years has edited *Die Fackel*, is very well known.⁶ On the whole, the contributions are of high caliber and interesting. Then there is the quite classic prose of the editorials.

1. George Reavey did not edit the English edition of *Formes*. Reavey, *Faust's Metamorphoses* (Fontenay-Aux Roses: New Review Editions, 1932).
2. Samuel Beckett, *Proust* (London: Chatto & Windus, 1931; New York: Grove Press, 1957).
3. Thomas McGreevy, *Thomas Stearns Eliot* (London: Chatto & Windus, 1931). McGreevy's book was reviewed by Robert Sage, "A Balanced Estimate of T. S. Eliot," *Chicago Tribune* (European edition), 8 February 1931, p. 5.
4. Gertrude Stein, *The Making of Americans* (Paris: Contact Editions, 1925; New York: Boni, 1926). Samuel Putnam, who was apparently Bald's friend "John", offers a slightly different account of this encounter with Stein in *Paris Was Our Mistress*, pp. 136–39 (see p. 40, n. 1). He notes that Stein referred not to *The Making of Americans*, but to *Three Lives* (New York: Grafton Press, 1909; London: John Lane/Bodley Head, 1915), her first book.
5. Wyndham Lewis writes, "The infantile is the link between the Superrealists and Miss Stein, as it is between Miss Stein and Miss Loos" ("The Diabolical Principle," in *The Enemy No. 3* [first quarter 1929], p. 41). This statement is also in Lewis's *The Diabolical Principle and The Dithyrambic Spectator* (London: Chatto & Windus, 1931; New York: Haskell House, 1971), p. 65.
6. Bald refers to *This Quarter*, 3.3 (January, February, March 1931). Karl Kraus edited *Die Fackel* in Vienna from 1899 until 1936.

Tuesday, 14 April 1931, p. 4.

They are talking about "White Magic."

In the cafés of Montparnasse, they are talking about "the new middle ages." They are talking about "the new objectivism" and the secrets of "Zang-tumb-tumb." There is another war.

The writers are fighting it out in the second issue of *The New Review*, published in Montparnasse, which appears this week. Samuel Putnam, Ezra Pound, Hilaire Hiler, George Antheil, Louis Zukofsky, Hermann Mueller, T. F. Tracy and Lincoln Gillespie are in the army.[1]

Samuel Putnam, in an exhaustive and esoteric exposé, wherein he scores the births and deaths of the "isms" since the war, traces the ancestry of the "Revolution of the Word." One might go back away behind the Renaissance. One might go to Aristotle, Quintilian or anywhere. The American champions of the word, says Putnam, are too late.

"As for the American-in-France self-advertised advance guard movement, it merely fastened parasitically upon the French. Their ideology is not to be taken seriously, but their seriousness is. The past decade was one of whiners, professional miaowlers."[2]

The champions in *The New Review* seem to agree on a discipline and clarity in letters. This makes for intelligibility and reconstruction. Emphasis is on the "object," on the sacramental significance of "reality."

Hilaire Hiler writes of the physiological appeal of art, scientific use of color, etc. See his drawings.

George Antheil discusses the physiological interest of contemporary music and the actuality of television for opera.

Lincoln Gillespie and T. F. Tracy write on the importance of clarity in literature. There is a new Link.

Ezra Pound drops bombs on his contemporaries and others. He doesn't waste words.

"Any bloke can experiment."

"O Jamie! thine epigons!"[3] What in the hell are "epigons"?

He explodes Harriet Monroe, Masters, Frost and company.

He offers a new definition for the word "bourgeois."

Here is an extract from a poem by George Kent, a brilliant newspaperman if there ever was one:

> I swing the water out of my toothbrush ja and rub my scalp
>   and cook my breakfast.
> But there are no more hairpins . . .
> Hey you bum . . . get a seamove on . . .
> It was like goats on nobody's mountain.
> There would always be one to tickle your hot back when you
>   fell into the bed.
> Sometimes I said, look here why aren't you more careful?
> Today, there are no more hairpins.[4]

The articles by various German, Spanish and French writers seem to bump, kick and bite. Richard Thoma, associate editor of *The New Review*, contributes the first chapter of his novel, *Tragedy in Blue*. The richest essay, "Rainer Maria Rilke," was written by Alfred Perlès. Some of the contributions are not hot at all, and one or two are without temperature. I liked Russel Wright's studies of Herbert Hoover, Mary Pickford and Greta Garbo.[5]

*
* *

1. *New Review*, 1.2 (May-June-July 1931), includes Samuel Putnam's "Black Arrow," pp. 71-82; Ezra Pound's "Our Contemporaries and Others," pp. 149-52, and "Definitions," p. 159; Hilaire Hiler's "Neonaturism" (with a note by George Antheil), pp. 89-91, and two paintings; Antheil's "Towards an American Music," pp. 112-18; Louis Zukofsky's " 'A' Third and Fourth Movements: 'Out of the Voices,' " pp. 83-88, and "Imagisme" (a review of René Taupin's *L'Influence du symbolisme français sur la poésie américaine*), pp. 160-61; Hermann Mueller's "Nachkrieg: A Letter from Germany," pp. 92-97; T. F. Tracy and Lincoln Gillespie's "Clarity in Literature," pp. 98-100. This number also includes Bald's "New Garters for Apollo," pp. 146-48.
2. Putnam, pp. 73-74.
3. The Pound quotations are, respectively, from pp. 151, 149.
4. George Kent, "There Are No Hairpins," *New Review*, p. 101.
5. This number of *New Review* also includes Richard Thoma's "Tragedy in Blue: The White Enigma," pp. 128-34; Alfred Perlès's "Rainer Maria Rilke," pp. 120-26; and photographs of Russel Wright's sculptures facing pp. 101, 119, 127.

Tuesday, 28 April 1931, p. 4.

I shall never forget the first time I met Maryse Choisy. It was in one of those sun-flooded studios overlooking the Place du Panthéon which only American millionaires can afford to own. Absolutely all of the Gold Coast society and the Long Island mob were there; the afternoon coats, *und so weiter*, were a bit overpowering, I must admit. Nevertheless, I could not help noticing over in a corner a certain lady whose hair was dark as Africa itself and whose eyes were darker still, if subsequent Montparnasse poets are to be credited.

I was on the point of remarking to my hostess, "Who is that in the corner?" Then there dashed across that sedate drawing room a young and beautifully-groomed lioness. From the corner of the room I heard: "O pet, what are you doing there?"

Whereupon I looked at my hostess and the stellar guests, who remarked: "It is only one of her desert pets."

In some astonishment, I looked at Maryse, who replied: "None of you know who I am! I am she who spent a month among the young ladies of Paris."

"Really!" exclaimed the group.

At that moment, the lioness ran up to lick the hand of a gentleman on the other side of the room. The gentleman in question was Joseph Delteil.

"Undoubtedly I have met you before," said I to the French writer.

Said he to me: "You are probably right. . . . I also met Maryse Choisy at a number of Montparnasse parties. I remember her Arctic smile, but perhaps she has forgotten me."

"Don't believe him," said Maryse. "I have known him since he was a famous writer. He may be a lion but you should have seen all the lions I shot in Africa. And if I haven't shot them, I will."

I looked at her and at the assembly. Everyone present respected the girl. The ex-wife of a diplomat, she staked everything on adventure. Her whole life was a gamble. She has written half a dozen novels, the details of which would shock an ordinary woman.

She wrote *Love in Prison*. For material, she managed to get pinched for soliciting. In St. Lazare, she learned about the unhappy women. Another book was *Advice to Women*. It tells them how.

"Tell me about your *Un Mois chez les filles*," I asked.

"That isn't important," said the novelist. "Let me tell you about *Un Mois chez les hommes.* That book tells about my experience with the monks on Mont Athos.[1] I was the first woman to get there. To get in that sacred colony, I hid in a mattress. What I learned was plenty! No female was permitted there. Anticipating a careful examination, I was armed with artificial credentials so cunningly devised that no one was the wiser."

She winked.

That was the woman—hungry for bundles of experience. Three days ago, she walked into the Coupole with a big bear. She loves animals. The photo entitled *Leda and the Snake* shows this woman with her favorite. She has her favorites. She is odd.

Peter Neagoe, one of the old *transition* group, threw the terraces into a tumult last night by announcing the forthcoming publication of an *American Abroad Anthology* (No. 1) edited by the *New Review* editions.[2]

"The anthology will be catholic in scope, without regard to literary politics or prejudices," he said. "It will cover the period between the Armistice to the Wall Street crash. It will include all the well-known Montparnasse luminaries such as Hemingway, McAlmon, Callaghan et al., and in addition all innocents abroad whose innocence has found an outlet in type in the last ten or twelve years."

*
* *

1. Maryse Choisy (Clouzet), *L'Amour dans les prisons* (Paris: Editions Montaigne, 1930); *Le tour du coeur en 80 battements* (Paris: Bernardin-Béchet, n.d.) *Un Mois chez les filles* (Paris: Editions Montaigne, 1928); *Un Mois chez les hommes* (Paris: Editions de France, 1929). For details about Choisy's visit to Mount Athos—and a picture of her dressed as a man—see "Disguised as a Man She Visits the Woman-Hating Hermits of Mt. Athos," *The American Weekly* (Sunday supplement to the Hearst newspapers), 12 April 1931, p. 3.
2. Peter Neagoe, ed., *Americans Abroad An Anthology* (The Hague: Servire, 1932). The volume includes Bald's "Dreary," pp. 8–18.

Tuesday, 5 May 1931, p. 4.

What about the pioneers?

I breathe hard whenever I think of those literary hermits who struggle in the south of France. Beyond the reach of glory, they live in solitude and slave their days away. For the love of creation, they ride their convictions through clouds of pink and do not complain. And such is the kingdom of heaven.

I am thinking of Lincoln Gillespie, Jr. His history reads like a Pindaric ode. Years ago he gave up a good job as a timekeeper in a million-dollar railroad company, where he was earning $22 a week with the promise of a bonus every fall. But dollars meant nothing. One day he told his boss: "A new word is as good as an old dollar."

That is the story of his life. Now this literary Gauguin lives on the brow of a bluff overlooking the Mediterranean. He writes poetry when the spirit pushes him, and nothing pleases him more than to whack the bushes of beauty for an elusive symbol. He likes to be employed about those regions which are never quite understood.

The following is an extract from one of his more recent achievements:

> Truth circumstance
> 'salways a gripe relish acefetidy
>   antitharmorplate
> to breath   strinct-scoriate   one's
>   fellociate
> in public
> And awksquirms?

Enter: Beard of Cullipodus.

A few days ago, the poet arrived in Paris with a chin string which he called "the beard of Cullipodus." Several hours later, while Link was asleep at the Dôme, a girl friend played a trick on him. With a nail file and a hairpin, she nipped the beard, and he no longer looks like Richelieu.

Said Link to his friends: "That woman is only a social rodent, a carniverous manapstasia. She used to rawk with sandatalama!" No one believed him, however.

They say about Link that he is capable of melting five words into an oath. He is reported to have stated that he can use seven images without the aid of grammar. The meanings are not always clear. Once he said: "My meanings are just around the corner." Link never talks; he lectures. The boys and girls at the Dôme hang on to his words with grim smiles. Listening would be less difficult if he didn't have a habit of reaching in his vest pocket every minute or so for a chunk of cheese. Nibbling cheese is Link's favorite soother. Years ago he said:

Joyceophalicosity.

"There are two great moderns and Joyce is getting old."

Yesterday afternoon, the word-maker was asleep at the Coupole. I grabbed his shoulders and shook him until he closed his mouth. I said: "Wake up, Link. I want to interview you." He opened his eyes, stared, and fell back into the subconscious. I squirted some seltzer down his neck and then shouted: "Pull yourself together, Link. This is an interview." Two gar-çons standing behind me were smiling at my efforts. Neither they nor Link appreciated the dignity of an interview. At last he woke up. A piece of cheese did it. I pulled it out of his pocket and held it to his face a full minute.

"I never give out interviews," said Link. A few minutes later he added: "Montparnasse writers are too loose! Why don't they tighten up their prose? What do you know about Dutch architecture or the geometric application of Sanscrit? I like the melodic lines of Epstein's work. The trouble with English and American women is that they have a strawy odor, because they don't eat enough vegetables. Order another *fine à l'eau.*"

Again he fell asleep. I picked him off the floor and set him on a chair.

About 7 o'clock I saw Link asleep at the Select. I woke him up and said: "Answer a few questions." He said: "Shall I be banal or would you like to hear a few Pizzikaks?" I said: "Mix them up." He said: "All right." Then it was my turn.

"What do you think of Beethoven?"

"Froghide croakboom legs for dinner."

"How do you react to Ravel?"

"Diamond dice thrown high."

"What is a Pizzivol?"

"Kissqueak fingplek daddleback."

"Will you ansamander one more questacdaquaff?"

"Poefix may ultraprovide anything!"

"Tellabel me this: Can you let me take 30 francs until tomorrow?"

Ambiblitheriticous.

"I haven't any money on me, but stick around and we'll borrow some together."

A little after midnight, Link was fast asleep in Jimmie's bar. I didn't have the heart to disturb him. As he lay there, whistling to himself, I thought of his psychological separation. To him words and word unions are like crawling animals. They are microscopic and fertile. "A new word is as good as an old dollar" and sometimes they are just around the corner.

I walked over to the recumbent figure and studied it. Protruding from one of its pockets was a sheet of paper. I drew it out and read "A Poem from Puzlit." The last lines clarified everything:

> sardonically towers
> ghoubrel
> i shing my ostracization
> come back!
> come back, I implore you
> no—stay away
> here
> i am ecstaticly.

Those lines will go down in the history of Montparnasse poets. They hold a cry and a weapon. Poor Link! As he lay there, asleep on the shelf, I wondered if his words slept too. What does he think about? Does anyone know? Does he know? Does anyone care?

Before my tears wash the ink off this copy, I shall close our panegyric with a love story. That story is old, but most of the stuff I write about is old.

Link had a girl. She loved him. He didn't mind. Came a day when he decided to have two women. He added a young peasant woman. . . . His girl was furious.

"Dismiss that woman," she said.

"My needs have increased," said the author of "Amerikaka."[1] "One and one make two."

Subadditorialization.

That night the vengeful paramour departed and took the rival with her. They went to Paris. Link was left alone. He found the following note pinned to the kitchen wall: "You thought that one and one make two. Well, one minus two make zero."

The deserted poet wired back: "One minus two rid me of you. Anyway, I was beginning to tire of your synthetic olfactory reprehensibility. Asyndic desertita yowlacat scrap finalapurgatude chainbind pettabibbletory. And I am glad of it."

*

1. See p. 25, n. 1.

Tuesday, 19 May 1931, p. 4.

MOUGINS (By Mail.)—

*
* *

Down in Venice, the D. H. Lawrence exhibit is still attracting visitors and comment. One of the Cagnes painters was given permission to varnish the lot after he had discovered that house paint had been used by Lawrence.

Bob Brown, dean of the Cagnes literati, is about to publish the manuscripts sent him for his "readies."[1] Among the contributors are William Carlos Williams, Norman Macleod, Samuel Putnam, Kay Boyle, Marinetti, Don MacKenzie, Ezra Pound and Gertrude Stein.

The idea of the "readies" is to publish books in microscopic type on a tape measure controlled by an electric motor. A magnifying glass enlarges the words as they roll through the machine. The purpose is to save time and space, and Bob thinks that a library can thus be carried in a small suitcase. The machine is in process of construction by Ross Saunders, of the same colony.

Someone suggested to Bob that Ronald Firbank's books be printed on lavender tape. Also that some appliance should release ducts of perfume to win the reader after each chapter. There are any number of possibilities. A writer asked Saunders to attach a microphone which will register the labor pains of composition. "The public should know."

*

1. *Readies for Bob Brown's Machine*, ed. Bob Brown (Cagnes-sur-Mer: Roving Eye Press, 1931).

Tuesday, 23 June 1931, p. 4.

Someone in the next apartment is playing the Victrola and the music is tickling my fancy. That music and this weather have given me thoughts; and when I get thoughts, I smoke many cigarettes. I have already smoked half a package but still can think of nothing significant. However—to plunge into problems.

What worries me most is the recurrent complaint that Montparnasse has died.

Has Bohemia folded? Is the Dôme just a café? Has the "lost generation" found itself? Is it true that mediocrity has whitewashed the Carrefour? If so, does it make any difference? All replies, if accompanied by a stamped envelope, will be considered.

They say that the grand old colony has become a rendezvous for loungers and fakirs, that the real people with their legends are hiding in limbo. Some are hiding in Villefranche.

The thinkers say that commerce is responsible. It is a fact that many people drop around to shop for shirts, flowers and fish. The fish stand of the Coupole is the worst taunt. It is like the last laugh or the last command or the last emotion in *The Blue Angel*, which, by the way, impressed me. I wish someone could induce Emil Jannings to stand in front of the Dôme and register the last gasp of Bohemia.

Let's get down to the bottom. I submit one testimonial: Mencken.

H. L. Mencken, when I interviewed him for the *Tribune*, said:

Montparnasse will never be a back number. I wish there were 100 of them in the world. There are more ideas there in a month than most professors have in a lifetime. What if there are fakirs in Montparnasse? That's all right. The world is full of fakirs. People in America are so full of inhibitions that they are afraid to be happy. Fakirs have color. If a fellow gets a kick out of growing a beard and playing with his subconscious to pass the time away, that's his privilege. What more is necessary? If he gets a girl to be his playmate, so much the better. But, my God, the taste some of those fellows have!

O. O. McIntyre, in a more recent interview, said:

I'll tell you: these terraces will always appeal to New Yorkers. They get a kick out of it if they don't stay too long. Where else can you sit all afternoon and see so many monkeys without having to meet them? Look at that guy. Look at that one. Every fifteenth man here is a story. Some of them must have fallen off the trees. Do you see that guy whose coat is patched with old newspapers? Someone must have picked up a stone and found him.

Christine Diemer was interviewed last Thursday as she was steering Vivian Duncan through the Quarter. Christine seems to know everyone in Paris, and her opinion is especially valuable because she climbed from a convent into a chorus and now she contributes both sides of the picture to *Variety*, that directory. Without a moment's hesitation, she said: "The Quarter is not shot to pieces. Don't you believe it for one solitary minute. Everyone comes here even if they don't stay long, and I'm getting a little tired of it myself."

Anna Stepney, the tall blonde actress who is singing at the new Palata, said: "Montparnasse is the only place from now on. It is the only place and even Montmartre thinks so."

Doris Carlyle, once the Queen of Greenwich Village, was of a different opinion. Doris knows life from many angles, having worked as a dancer, hash slinger and mule driver. Years ago, she was the treat of many Village boys and imbibed their philosophy. She was emphatic:

Montparnasse is just a bubble blown wrong. It used to be different, but now there are no bones left in the garbage can. What do you mean, atmosphere! This side of the fence never did smell right. All that's left is just a bunch of pikers, anyway. The real gang have gone forever. And I don't mean if.

That Victrola on the other side of the wall is still bothering me. They have been playing the same tune about 50 times. I am going to move out of this place anyway. Every time I try to think, a bunch of school kids stand out in the court yard and yell. Yesterday they parked there all afternoon and played nine-pins.

But let me tell this one about a well-known Quarter type who probably won't live long. Her real name doesn't matter—we'll call her Quelquefois Sonia. This daughter of impulse sits in sullen frigidity on the terrace of the Coupole every afternoon. Her red hair is caught by a green hat which she often slaps in despair. Sometimes she slaps the table or the chair. Once I saw her slap five men in rapid succession.

Two years ago, she loved a preacher. He gave her the gate. She went wild. Booze and revelry. At night, she goes to the dance halls in the Latin Quarter.

Often she dances alone. Sometimes she dances with other girls. She will not dance with any man. That is her situation.

Tragedy changed that girl. She is often discovered telling her troubles to other girls and she tells them that an early suicide is her only enthusiasm. When asked her reaction to Montparnasse, she replied that she didn't care where she lived. She added, however, that she'd be damned if she'd die there.

*

Tuesday, 28 July 1931, p. 4.

*
* *

We have in our possession Bob Brown's latest volume of poetry. Bob, the author of *Words* and *Gems*, is one of the deans of Cagnes. His last volume, *Demonics*, has so much verve and elan that we were tempted to quote several pages, skipping of course the short but honest words.

Bob is a slack-wire performer without a parasol. In his "Amurica I Luve You," he rattles off the Yankee traditions in coarse but effulgent idiom. His stuff hits and bites. Perhaps he is a Paycock searching for a Juno. His coined phrases yawp and slaughter his pets. How do you like this from "Spring, Put on a . . ."?

> In your fur-nuzzle
>> incubate Eskimo eggs
>> hot-sand baby crocodiles
>> to slimy long
>> navel-stringed birth
>> Set on pickled Chinese eggs. . . .

But a better example is the following insult to the moon:

>> . . . Haunter of cemeteries
>> pal of prowling cats
>> noser of garbage
>> sneaking satellite
>> even the dogs howl at you.

Some readers will not accept this total disregard of form. Others find such material highly entertaining. *Demonics* was published by the Roving Eye Press.[1]

*
*   *

1. Bob Brown, *Words* (Paris: Hours Press, 1931); *Gems: A Censored Anthology* (Cagnes-sur-Mer: Roving Eye Press, 1931); *Demonics* (Cagnes-sur-Mer: Roving Eye Press, 1931). Bald refers to Brown's "Amurica I Luve You," *Demonics*, pp. 6–8, and quotes from "Spring, Put on a Condom!" *Demonics*, p. 7, and "Bellowing at the Moon," *Demonics*, p. 23. In the second excerpt Bald omits "peerer into ash-cans" from between his second and third lines.

Wednesday, 12 August 1931, p. 4.

The uncrowned Queen of the Dôme has packed her bags. The Countess is going away. Her influence may stagger on, but her spot will not be filled again in this colony. She was its most persistent Bohemian.

In future years, the passing of the Countess will indicate to the historians the end of an era. Montparnasse has had so many eras that it will not be easy to decide which one this is. Most of our contemporaries have called it the last one and run away to other districts. If this emigration continues nothing will remain but a legend and half a dozen crowded saloons. Destiny.

At any rate, visitors to the Quarter were always received by this gracious ennui dodger whose informal tours of the bars were conducted with simplicity and decorum. Her voice had a churning lilt that at odd moments carried all before her. Ever after they would bow to her, especially from a distance. Such was her charm and even the way she grinned was dramatic. The Countess was an unqualified Bohemian because her ego never emerged. It never questioned her libido.

On the eve of her departure old stories come drifting back—her escapades and epigrams. About the time when she ran into Michael Arlen at the Falstaff and made it clear that she too was a babe in the woods and that he didn't look so grown-up himself. About the time when she lectured ten policemen for not running her in. About the time when she sprang onto a table at the Select and did a clog dance. About the time when she consoled three homesick sailors. About the time when she rushed, white-faced and breathless, into Jimmie's bar and announced that she had decided to settle down to writing books. About the time when she led a parade of artists from the Left Bank to the Right. And how she led them back again at the urgent request of the invaded territory. But the barmen of Montparnasse will miss her most.

Let the Countess tell her own story:

I was born in London of Australian parents. My antecedents were statesmen. At the age of 13 I rode horseback and bust my complacency. Of course I was very high-strung but never neurotic until I came to Montparnasse. At 17 I played the piano divinely and landed on the London Hippodrome at 22. There I did a single turn and sang Elsie Janis songs. In 1926 I was divorced and paid for it. All I have left is philosophy.

The above account gives the barest details of a vivid career. Moreover, her personality must be felt rather than explained. Many will agree. When she leaves Montparnasse her background, so indispensable, will be destroyed.

Why is she going away?

For the past two or three weeks the Countess was detained at St. Lazare. A debate with a taxi driver was responsible. Then she was urged to leave for London.

"It was all due to a misunderstanding," said the Countess. "I shall never quite forget St. Lazare. They herded me with a sordid crowd. Murderers and wild tigers. The brown bread was so solid that you could kill a man with it. Some of that crowd was so dirty that the crawlers wouldn't touch them. But I could bear anything if it weren't for my spiritual trouble."

Whatever they say about the Countess, she has more courage than most of her critics. Perhaps she will breathe her fire upon Soho or Chelsea. London will have something to contend with and may profit by her irrepressible genius. She may plant a new colony.

*
* *

Wednesday, 19 August 1931, p. 4.

The birth of *The New Review* in Montparnasse started something six months ago. It dared to peep with clarity at the new possibilities and the old horses neighed their disapproval. All the more fun!

But Montparnasse is on its toes now. They are getting hot. The third number of *The New Review* (whose major contributors are Parnassians) is the talk of the Quarter.

Well may it be. The articles which constitute half the magazine are the weakest gibberish of this decade. Berl, with his outmoded "Unconscious" and tardy annihilation of Bergson, makes one giggle. Ferrero's absorption in the problem of art is too collegiate for comment. And Bodenheim *will* be a social climber.[1]

Very sorry is the exhibition of Unamuno whose "How to Write a Novel" is merely a diary charged with hysteria.[2] We have no patience with an inflated lyric embedded in cement. Such naked screams should make you blush. Such bubble protests of neurasthenia are immodest.

Saddest of all is the contribution of Andrei Biely, the Russian, whom somebody dubbed the Russian Joyce.[3] That somebody should be condemned to remain a frustrated critic until the end of his decline. Biely is a corrupt Dostoevski who was confused by metaphysics and sank into the more comfortable medium of literature. He screams on the brink of an era of epilepsy and sadism. His colossal mysticism is the fantasy of a padded cell. He couldn't even write editorials for a small town newspaper. No one is interested in that man's elusive soul. The other little essays are waste.

And yet the third number of *The New Review* is the best to date. It is carried by its fiction. The short stories and chapter extracts of novels have brought to the fore a number of brilliant young writers, each of whom shows astonishing fertility and inventiveness. Most interesting of all is the range. The gap between James Farrell's "Jewboy" and Richard Thoma's "Tragedy in Blue" is wide.[4] The former is a slice of life by an artist whose work shows crudity at its best. The latter stands head over heels above the other contributors of *The New Review*.

Thoma's mastery of form, his ability to finger brocades of words and squirt perfumes, reveals a decadence that is curiously redolent of Flaubert and reminiscent of Huysmans. His metaphors are bizarre and pulling. They smell of musk and other content.

Henry Miller's study of a *maquereau* is unique as an exploitation of a guileless worm. Its sustained objectivity is an achievement. Alfred Perlès contributes an explosive, subjective microcosm of fantasy that will be hailed as the closest thing to excellence. Peter Neagoe's story shows the former *transition* creator at his best.[5]

The editor, Samuel Putnam, offers a poem that should explain something of its creator. Ida Graves, an English girl discovered by one of the contributors, offers two unusual nuggets.[6]

All in all, the contributions are very good and very bad. *The New Review* is speeding ahead.

*
* *

1. *New Review*, 1.3 (August-September-October 1931), includes Emmanuel Berl's "The Bankrupcy of the Unconscious," pp. 84–86; Léo Ferrero, "Leonardo, or the Problem of Art," pp. 64–72; Maxwell Bodenheim's "Esthetics, Criticism, and Life," pp. 100–107. It also includes Bald's "Dreary," pp. 50–58.
2. Miguel de Unamuno, "How to Write a Novel," *New Review*, pp. 13–20.
3. Andrei Biely, "Kotik Letaev," *New Review*, pp. 32–38.
4. This number of *New Review* includes James T. Farrell's "Jewboy," pp. 21–26, and Richard Thoma's "Tragedy in Blue: The Nightingale Sings," pp. 87–97.
5. Also included in this number of *New Review* are Henry Miller's "Mademoiselle Claude," pp. 39–45; Alfred Perlès's "Title to Follow: A Novel," pp. 76–82; and Peter Neagoe's " 'They,' " pp. 27–30.
6. Samuel Putnam contributed "As Browning Would Have Said" to this number of *New Review*, pp. 60–62; Ida Graves provided "Two Poems" ("The Birth of Abel" and "Identity"), p. 83.

Wednesday, 2 September 1931, p. 5.

*
* *

Djuna Barnes, author of *Ryder*, returned to Montparnasse for a glimpse and fled to Vienna. . . .[1]

"Montparnasse," she said, "has ceased to exist. There is nothing left but a big crowd."

"Don't put it that way," I said. "I love the Quarter."

Then we rested our heads on each other's shoulders and wept for a minute. Djuna is well built and has a rich, red ocean of hair. We swapped anecdotes and had tea.

"Do you remember—?" she said.

"Yes. And how about—?"

That went on for about an hour.

Djuna took an apartment in the Rue St. Romain, far from the present bluster. She told me it was all over.

"Montparnasse is all over," she said. "And Greenwich Village is all over. It's all all over."

I protested. "You're teasing me," I said.

"It's all over in New York," she added. "Two weeks before the end of the *World*, I was spreading a high class Winchell.[2] For what? That is all over now."

Everything is all over. Djuna heard me with frigidity. Everyone knows that that was all over before it started. We had more tea.

A girl I once knew in Chicago came into the room. "Is this interview all over?" she said.

Then the three of us had more tea and we talked about the post-War days when Bohemians pranced in circles and no one cared. I looked upon Djuna as a recovered hope. We agreed that it was all over.

*
* *

1. Djuna Barnes, *Ryder* (New York: Liveright, 1928).
2. Barnes refers to her "Knickerbocker Almanac 1931," in *The World Magazine* (Sunday supplement to the *New York World*), 8 February 1931, p. 2; 22 February 1931, p. 2. The *World* last appeared on 27 February 1931.

Wednesday, 9 September 1931, p. 5.

*
* *

A letter from Luis Buñuel, creator of *Un Chien Andalou* and *L'Age d'Or*, daring surrealistic films.[1] He writes from Moscow that there is great hope for the free film in Soviet Russia, despite the burden of propaganda. This man, formerly a student of philosophy at a Spanish University, is against culture, education and, particularly, religion. He is one of the Spanish irritants who make a habit of writing manifestoes. Before making his trip to Russia he told me that Hollywood is quite hopeless.

June Mansfield will be back in a couple of weeks. This should interest those who know June and her temperament. When she left last October she said she wanted to start her novel, *Happier Days*. She writes that the job is completed.[2] In New York, June ran a Bohemian hell-hole called the Fire Bird. It had a Stravinsky setting. The decor was executed by Jean Kronski, one of her friends who is now reported to be living in an insane asylum. At least three or four men are said to have committed suicide for love of June. Among them was a famous acrobat whose attacks were very awkward. They say that she repulsed him frequently and that he brooded for a long while.

*

1. Luis Buñuel's films include *Un Chien Andalou* (1929) and *L'Age d'Or* (1930).
2. June Mansfield published no book.

Wednesday, 7 October 1931, p. 4.

Cagnes unloads Lincoln Gillespie on Montparnasse again. I asked him for a complete account of his best adventure in the last six months.

He said that he ran into Henry Rothschild II in front of the Miramar two months ago.

"So," said Link, "we strolled nonchalantly to a table laden with Spanish beauties and Miss Chicago. All the tables were filled with high society. We were surrounded by the upper flotilla with the exception of one gigolo—a Spanish duke. I almost had hemorrhages."

Link is back for about ten days. He said that he didn't mind the long train ride because he was chaperoning two virgins from Cagnes. He is very popular in Montparnasse and even the garçons eyed him questioningly. In the picture, he is sitting behind Francis Dickie. I asked him to finish his story.

> Well, we were all sitting there when suddenly I observed that two cordial necks were turning in my direction from the next table. One was Michael Arlen whom I never saw before and the other was Noel Coward. I walked up and told Mr. Arlen, whom I recognized by photograph, that he interested me. I said "Mr. Arlen, I have been following your work for some years now although I missed the last one. I think of you and Ronald Firbank as compeerlesshiness in this realm. I appreciate the fanswichclaxbeck of your chiaroscuro."

Link tells a story very well. He lingers over the details. I liked the way he said: "Mr. Arlen, you have probably never met me before. I am Gillespie of *transition.*" Arlen immediately introduced him to Coward and finished his drink.

Link also told me that "Coward had to suppute that his friend Arlen was several notches higher in the literary realm than he had not suspected."

Link Gillespie is a cheerful guy.

*

Wednesday, 14 October 1931, p. 4.

Even in this barren age with its economic problems, romance is just around the corner. Indeed, adventure waits at night in the dark streets of Paris.

Night before last all the stars were out and I was walking very slowly to appreciate their beauty. Occasionally a painted smile tried to block my way, but I wandered on and on under the big stars. And looking at a full moon often gives me an emotion.

Near the shadows of the Louvre a lone figure began to follow me and tapped me on the shoulder after a short chase. He was dressed in corduroy, a gray jacket and thick spectacles. His hat was carelessly jammed on one side of his head and the uncovered side was quite bald. It was Henry Miller, the novelist.

"Hello," I said. We talked about this and that and smoked a few cigarettes. Then I said: "Where are you going?"

He replied: "Nowhere in particular."

That's just like Miller. He is never definite. Miller has been out of a job for some time and he hasn't a cent. But he's lucky. He has friends. They always take care of him.

A couple of days ago he woke up on a bench outside the Closerie des Lilas. The only thing that bothered him, he said, was that he didn't have a toothbrush. "Being on the bum is all right if you can clean your teeth occasionally—say, every third day. Otherwise you feel bad."

But he doesn't worry. His friends are always backing him up. The other day he met Kann the sculptor, who has just landed a fat contract from America. They dined at Ciro's. During the meal Miller reached in his pocket for a handkerchief and pulled out a pair of socks. At Ciro's! In the evening he met another friend, Joe Chock. Joe has just broken into Broadway with a burlesque on heaven. It's a radio play. The hero goes around through five acts with a microphone concealed in his *caleçons*. Miller likes friend Joe because the latter drinks champagne and smokes Coronas. Miller showed me a few of the butts he had collected. Succulent snipes. He smokes only the best butts when he is with Joe.

"Then what?" I asked in a loud voice because Miller was falling asleep on his feet. He hadn't slept for two nights.

"I don't have to worry about a job. In Montparnasse no one has to work. The next day I met another friend of mine. You know, Ludwig Truss, the butter and egg producer. At four in the morning, after a long discussion about life and travel, he took me for a long drive in his Suiza to Fontaine-bleau. The mist was rising from the lake and the ducks were very white. We sat on a terrace overlooking the palace of François Ier. Then we argued about how many horses one could drive abreast up the crazy stairs of the palace. But we both got bored and began to drive back to Paris. We had a big breakfast at the Dôme."

"What a wonderful life!" I said.

"That's how it is," said Miller. "Other friends came up. They look high and low for me. There's Osman the banker, who always treats me to sparkling Mousseux. I shake hands with people all day long. Even Link Gillespie once bought me a drink. Montparnasse is a great place. Everyone likes to help a fellow who is broke. A couple of days ago, a girl I hardly knew stopped me on the street. I told her about my status, so she took me home with her and sewed a couple of buttons on my coat and trousers. People are swell, do you see what I mean? They worry about you."

I am reporting our conversation very faithfully. Miller is not a son of badinage. He is a legitimate child of Montparnasse, the salt of the Quarter. He represents its classic color that has not faded since Murger and other optimists. A good word is *esprit*. I told him that. "You have *esprit*," I said, lighting his cigar butt. Then he said: "Can you give me an alarm clock?"

"What for?"

"Well, you see, Joe," (He always calls me Joe. He calls everybody Joe.) "I am having such a good time that I hate to miss any of it. I like to get up early to enjoy every available hour."

Suddenly Miller staggered and fell back against the wall of a building. "What's the matter?" I said. His voice was frail and I could read between the lines of his face.

"What you need is food," I said, reaching in my pocket. "I'm your friend, too. Get yourself some food," I said, and handed him a franc.

Montparnasse is that way.

*
* *

Tuesday, 3 November 1931, p. 4.

The bored are occasionally treated to a rumor that Aleister Crowley is back in Montparnasse. Then there is a thrill and new conversation.

These rumors are false and the notorious sorcerer has just sent us a letter to prove it. A couple of years ago he was asked to get out of the country, and since then a dozen sensational legends have reached a suggestible public, all of them more or less plausible and decidedly nutritious.

Possibly the best story was his interesting "suicide" in Portugal about nine months ago. On one bank of a raging whirlpool called "The Mouth of Hell" was found the following note signed by our former neighbor: "Your mouth was hotter than this," addressed obviously to a woman. After that he was reported to be in Hollywood, in Moscow and in Cicero. One story had him lecturing at Cornell on ethics and eugenics.

At any rate, Montparnasse cannot forget this romantic figure who used to stroll to the Dôme or the Coupole in kilties or plus fours, his entire head cleanly shaved save for a single waxed forelock described by himself as "the Mark of Buddha." Sometimes he called it his "Cling-Clong," and he was in the habit of dyeing it pink or saffron to explain his mood.

The author of *The Diary of a Drug Fiend* boasted of his skill in hypnotism and alchemy, an accomplishment that never fails to impress certain types of neurotic American women who feel themselves unfulfilled and suddenly discover a craving for a new content before surrendering to the inevitability of patient desolation.[1]

Crowley was a cheerful individual who would say to all comers: "I am a practicing magician." At his studio parties he would turn on green lights, murmur a few incantations and then perform a series of feats that never failed to entertain. There was nothing like it anywhere else in Montparnasse. And there is the story of his eugenic colony in Sicily, where perfect children were being manufactured until Mussolini got tired of it and told him to go away. It seems that quality is seldom respected.

And yet the intelligent have always regarded Crowley as a man of creative imagination and genuine enthusiasm for a poetic revaluation of amusement. He is also a painter, and at present he is exhibiting his work in Berlin. He writes: "Let me know if you have anything on hand that might wish to sympathize with fallen grandeur." His best painting is called *Three Men Carrying a Black Goat Across the Snow to Nowhere,* an ambiguous title but a positive indication of a good poet.

Black magic in Montparnasse is still being fostered by Mme. Maria de Naglowska, a handsome Russian woman who furthers her cause by peddling her own newspaper, *La Flèche,* in front of the Rotonde.[2] One night a week her flock gathers in a large, bare room not far from the Closerie des Lilas, and mild experiments are made. Another modern struggle with 19th century romanticism.

I spoke of all this to Bill Seabrook, the explorer and author of *The Magic Island* and *Jungle Ways.*[3] Bill is at home in Africa or Toulon, but he never fails to visit his old spot in the Place de l'Odéon, an affinity of 15 years standing.

This son of a preacher studied philosophy at college, read his father's Bible and finally rushed to the wild jungles for explanations. He found plenty and his recital of savage rites and mores was so startling that I bit off the end of my cigarette and gulped it down.

"Bill," I said, "you're a cannibal."

"You bet."

"Did you really eat human flesh at one of the jungle parties?"

"Sure."

"Was the victim a man, woman or child?"

"I don't know. They gave me a slice of neck."

"Did it taste like pork?"

"Yes, except that it needed more seasoning."

"Ugh!"[4]

And so I said to Bill: "Come along with me and I'll show you something in our own alley."

Bill took off his goatskin bathrobe and African sandals. He dressed and shaved, and followed me out of the house. We walked past the Place St.

Michel and past the Sorbonne neighborhood. The streets were dark. Finally we came to a shack and I glued my mouth to a keyhole. "Désespéré," I whispered hoarsely.

Someone opened the door and we walked down a long courtyard. So we descended two flights of cement stairs and I knocked cautiously on a dirty window after repeating the password.

We were admitted after some minutes and saw two men playing billiards with human skulls. "These men," I told Bill later, "are members of the Désespérés Club, a very eclectic circle." Then we went to the Dôme. But what got me sore was that Bill wasn't even impressed.

*
* *

1. See p. 33, n. 2.
2. *La Flèche. Organe d'action magique* was published in Paris from October 1930 until sometime in 1933.
3. William B. Seabrook, *The Magic Island* (New York: Harcourt, Brace, 1929; London: Harrap, 1929); *Jungle Ways* (New York: Harcourt, Brace, 1931; London: Harrap, 1931).
4. According to Marjorie Worthington, *The Strange World of Willie Seabrook* (New York: Harcourt, Brace & World, 1966), pp. 54–55, Seabrook did not eat human flesh in Africa; instead, he ate the flesh of a man who had been killed in a traffic accident in Paris.

Tuesday, 24 November 1931, p. 4.

Society on this side of the river had a big time last Saturday night. It was quite an occasion.

The younger set was invited to a dance recital at the home of Princess Lieven, a gracious and charming hostess with a brilliant lineage and flair for conversation.[1] The event, so to speak, was superabundant with pulchritude; and history informs us, not without unction, that the smart galas of the pre-Queen Anne *siècle* lacked the flavor of our own modest Left Bank whoopee.

Last year the same dancer gave a show at the same place.[2] It was that way again last Saturday. Everyone had a swell time. She is a good dancer. Her name is Helba Huara and she comes from Peru. She has a husband. His name is Gonzalo More. He was there too. He played the piano. When Helba

Huara dances I can hear the pleading of my soul's lost empires and I kneel to the pageant of reconstructed images while my nerves lunch from a cornucopia.

Prominent among the guests were: Clara Candiani, French poetess; Vincent Korda, designer and brother-in-law of the famous film star, Maria Korda; Blin, French film critic; Baroness Wittinghof; Chief Oscomon, American Indian; George Reavey, Irish poet; and Menkès.

Also prominent were Lajos Tihanyi, Hungarian painter; Mary Coles, American painter; Adolf Dehn, another painter; Bill Hayter, another painter; Mme. Lazare, another painter; and Brassaï, another painter.

A word about Helba. Two years ago, she starred in the Broadway hit, *A Night in Spain*.[3] After sweeping America she is now sweeping Europe, and she is still young. I am enthusiastic about her work.

The studio is big and austere. Electric lights were extinguished and the kerosene lamps threw eerie strips of shadow in all directions. The guests sprawled informally over assorted mattresses placed side by side in neat rows on the floor.

Helba is in a direct line from royal Inca blood and she was trained by Nijinsky in South America. She is the only Inca dance-revivalist, and she creates her own legends, costumes and music. Her inspiration is the fruit of her mother's teaching and research work in museums. Rites and legends are her prompters; she has drunk *chika*, talked the old Kichua tongue and played the *kena*, an instrument made of human bones. Her dancing is quite literary.

The guests left very late. Overcoats were piled in a heap about three feet high; and there was some commotion when it was discovered that underneath all those overcoats a baby was asleep. Add that nobody seemed to know whose property the baby was. There was some whispering and much concern over this situation for about half an hour. Then the rightful owner appeared from upstairs. Apologetic, he explained that he was so overcome by the excitement of the evening that he had retreated to knock off some poetry.

You should have seen Helba do the Granada, the Belle sans Bras, the Woman with a Funeral Bouquet, the Leper of the Spirit of Medieval Spain. She works with thumb drums; and she wore a funny bird hat, feathers and barbaric garters. The swastika may have been fished up from Lake Titicaca. Each dance was a narrative told by nuanced means and jiggling muscles. I wish I could dance like that.

*
* *

1. The spelling of Princess Désirée's surname is uncertain. Bald has Leven, but Mura Dehn, who knew her, says Lieven (letter to me, 12 May 1985), as does Henry Miller (*Tropic of Cancer* ms., p. 100, container 23 of the Huntington Cairns Papers, Library of Congress). Virginia Gardner uses Liven in *"Friend and Lover" The Life of Louise Bryant* (New York: Horizon Press, 1982), pp. 269, 359 n. 17.
2. See pp. 47-48.
3. Helba Huara appeared in A *Night in Spain* in 1927.

Tuesday, 22 December 1931, p. 4.

Tito Schipa, the tenor recently feted and decorated in Paris, is being sued for 20,000 francs by the Contessa Lina Monici, matron saint of Montparnasse. It is a delicate story.

"We were great friends," said the Contessa, who never exaggerates. "We sang together side by side in Milan many years ago. Puccini introduced us. Every time he comes to Paris I invite him to be my guest. I am still a good singer, but painting is my weakness now." She pointed to the oils and aquarelles on the wall.

I look admiringly at the lady. The demon of creation gallops through her veins. She can paint, sing, act, weep, scream and joke. She throws the best cocktail parties on this side of the river. She is so dynamic that her moods explode within her, and she can throw a whole café into a hush or a panic with a spontaneous gesture. Like the time I accidentally spilled some hot coffee on her lap and she got up and chased me all the way from the Select to a passing street car, which I luckily caught on the fly. She is also a good runner.

"Why are you suing your friend Schipa?" I asked. This business of asking personal questions I shall never outgrow. When I was a small boy, one of the teachers came up to my desk and pulled my ears and then sent me home. All I had said was: "Was that you near the boathouse last night?" Her name was Miss Swanson.

"Because he engaged me to paint his portrait," said the Contessa, "and he never paid the bill. He posed only once and refused to pose again. He broke appointment after appointment. I was obliged to finish the picture from memory and photographs, but he left for America without paying me. He was angry because I had painted his elbow on a piano. 'I am a singer, not a composer,' he said. *Il n'est pas gentil.*"

At once, her eyes melted and her cheeks were covered with tear-flakes.

"Don't cry, Lina," I crooned. "Most artists are unhappy." I get very tender once in a while.

"Schipa," she said finally, wiping my drenched shoulder with a towel, "doesn't remember the hard days of our youth. How he ran around with a celluloid collar and fancy shoes. He doesn't remember the time I complained that he was so covered with sweet-smelling musk that he reminded me of the fragrant potato barrels of Milan."

Then I pointed to an interesting individual in a black frock. He was singing to himself as he mixed the drinks. The other 20 or 30 guests were watching him, too.

"Who is that guy?" I asked.

"That," said Captain Paterson, Lina's husband, "is Angelo, an unfrocked priest. When the creditors arrive he talks to them in Latin, which discourages them. He is very useful here."

I looked at the rest of the crowd: artists, bankers, actors, a few journalists, vague elderly American women, widows, virgins, literary eunuchs croaking about new schools, penniless barons, and a wonderful blonde who speaks Hungarian. Maud Loty, a French actress, was preparing the coffee. Of all places on earth, only Montparnasse can offer such an aggregation, and only the Contessa Monici can assemble them within an hour. And they say the Quarter is dead. Montparnasse has been dying for many years, but its death rattle will survive this generation. It will survive this column, at least, and it won't have to wait very long. This damn old earth needs a sewer for its ambition.

*
* *

Tuesday, 29 December 1931, p. 4.

Christmas brought back Laurence Vail, surrealistic painter and writer of horror stories. We missed his pink shirt and corduroy pants but we heard a lot about his chateau in Villefranche. The Villefranche retreat is considerably enlivened by Vail's exciting murals: shooting stars, amorous fish, headless cans, falling towers, grinning tulips. Within its spacious corridors the elect of Villefranche stroll to and fro: Marcel Duchamp, Kay Boyle, Alfred Kreymborg, Nina Wilcox Putnam, Sindbad.

For a number of years Laurence has been famous for his agile subconsciousness, and his last novel, *Murder! Murder!*, is richly polluted with dream fantasies.[1] The style is agreeable and the plot wanders here and there. It tells about a man who is foully murdered but he doesn't believe in his own murder—so he wants to commit suicide to prove he is alive. That's the height of scepticism.

*
* *

Kay Boyle is back on the Avenue du Maine for the holidays. She has graduated from the little magazines to *Scribner's, Harper's* and *The New Yorker.* Her stuff is good. A warm reception was given her novel, *Plagued by the Nightingale,* which describes the plight of a sensitive woman who gets caught in matrimony, and her irritation therefrom. Kay said her next novel will be called *Year Before Last.*[2]

*
* *

Francis Dickie, veteran Canadian journalist and author, is writing another, the nature of which is a mystery.[3] Dickie says he labors 12 hours a day.

Dick Thoma offers *Green Chaos* to discouraged voluptuaries. The poems are exquisite blasphemies and every third line contains a symbol. We were particularly moved by the introduction:

> This is the end of the beginning of the proem
> and if you don't like it, you know what you can do—

—a brutal challenge to any reader.

The volume is recommended for its display of 1940 words like "smaragds," "crotals," "bulbus," "baobabs," "sex," "Mishach," "sagittally," "Ygdrasil," "farewell."

Occasionally the lines make the sympathetic reader wince with charred memories:

> Did you ever play as a child? Did you
> ever hide in dark places?
> Then forget where they were and search
> for them through your tears?

Baudelaire was dull as a policeman by contrast with:

> Sometimes I tear at her mouth with my fingers
> And lacerate her scrofulous thighs.
> Then, her hands are swifter than daggers
> And her rhythms are mingled with cries.

There are salient references to female scorpions and Greek gods, vapid women and exalted sailors. There are lines especially in "Fin du Monde" that rally in a maddening crescendo, wherein the effete singer hurls his defy and asks the world to swoon with him.[4] But the world doesn't rotate that fast.

Art for Americans.

Forty-five American artists will hold their first big show at the Galerie de la Renaissance, beginning January 18. Both Left and Right wings will be represented, and Chil Aronson, the organizer, predicts that this exhibit will be revived annually. Unlike other shrewd boosters, Aronson appears to be incapable of insincerity or tomato publicity.

Almost every Left Bank writer we can think of—good, bad and hopeless— will be represented in Bob Brown's forthcoming anthology.[5] The contributions will have a special value because of their informality, brevity and other features to be mentioned anon. Bob Brown's Readies, an infernal mechanical device, has had them buzzing for months. Imagine reading a book in 10 minutes!

Here is a partial list of contributors to this literary olio: William Carlos Williams, Donal MacKenzie, Nancy Cunard, Walter Lowenfels, Gertrude Stein, Norman Macleod, Hilaire Hiler, Manuel Komroff, Paul Bowles, F. T. Marinetti, Ezra Pound, Kay Boyle, Bob McAlmon, Lincoln Gillespie, Eugene Jolas, Laurence Vail, Charles Henri Ford, John Banting, Daphne Carr, Carlton Brown, George Kent, Rue Menken.

*

1. See p. 13, n. 1.
2. Kay Boyle wrote frequently for magazines. See, for example, "His Idea of a Mother," *Scribner's*, 90.1 (July 1931), pp. 73–77; "The First Lover," *Harper's*, 163 (June 1931), pp. 33–36; "Kroy Wen," *The New Yorker*, 7.23 (25 July 1931), pp. 13–15.

Boyle, *Plagued by the Nightingale* (New York: Cape & Smith, 1931; London: Cape, 1931); *Year Before Last* (New York: Harrison Smith, 1932; London: Faber & Faber, 1932).

3. Francis Dickie's only books are *The Master Breed* (New York: Doran, 1923) and *Umingmuk of the Barrens* (London: Hodder & Stoughton, 1927).

4. Richard Thoma, *Green Chaos* (Fontenay-aux-Roses, Seine, France: New Review Press, 1931). Bald quotes from "Poem for R.," p. 5; "Again for R.," p. 20; "Venus Maledicta," p. 16. "Fin du Monde" appears on pp. 31–33.

5. See p. 67, n. 1. Bald contributed "Flow Gently" to *Readies for Bob Brown's Machine*, pp. 60–61.

Tuesday, 12 January 1932, p. 4.

She wears the mask of death and her ghastly beauty makes them stare. She crosses the street and walks into the Select. An audience is born. Montparnasse is just a stage for June Mansfield.

There is something shadowy, drugged, about her speech; and when she talks to you, the ground slips from under your feet. She creates a certain atmosphere of unreality and you feel that her words lift you in a cloud of incense and leave you without a ladder. I was fascinated by her colorless face.

"What kind of powder do you use?" I asked, with the cynicism of a journalist.

"I am using Rachel No. 2," she answered, candidly.

Her hair is generally pinned high in back, or she lets it fly in the wind. Last year her hair was purple, the year before it was mauve, next year it will be platinum. Now it is dyed a gold-kissed rust, almost red. Her eyes are wide apart and very deep, like a pair of tawny pits. And I admired her anaconda throat.

"People hate me because I destroy them," June said. "I awaken their slumbering vices. Destruction may be very beautiful." She added that she considered herself a female Stavrogin. The mask grinned at me, and I felt very shy.

She has been on the stage, of course. Theatre Guild and Provincetown.[1] Once she almost doubled for Norma Talmadge, but the janitress notified her of the appointment three days too late. American concierges are pretty bad, too. At present, she carries her stage with her.

But I was interested in her conversation. Her speech consists of rapid monologues and her words travel faster than news reels. She flits from topic to topic with the grace of a bullet, and her monologues are like prairie fires. They are prairie fires that devastate great tracts of unimportance. She uses words like "succubus" and "necrophilian."

"Tell me more," I said.

"You are very young," she declared, disapprovingly. "I prefer to talk to men over 30. And you don't look sincere." We had an argument and I threatened to go home. Our eyes exchanged cautious silences for a minute, and then I reassured her: "I'm not mad at you."

"Let me," she said, warmly, "tell you about a mistake I once made. One day I was visiting the Paul Rosenberg Galleries. Two men approached me. They were Cocteau and Picasso. They introduced themselves. 'Get away!' I said. 'You're just a couple of imposters.' They went away, and when I learned later that they were really the ones, it was very funny. It was their misfortune."

"Tell me another story," I said.

"All right. Once I went swimming in the nude in the Seine. The police arrested me, and I was obliged to dress while we walked to the commissariat. They were amused when I drew their caricatures and they let me go. I was arrested not for swimming but for disturbing the slumber of the house-boaters."

It is evident that June is one of those modern women who choose to ride their impulses. This way of living often leads to complexities. The keynote of her nature is extravagance, a natural complement to incoordination. When her funds are low she will live for days on bread and butter, and wash it down with champagne. If the grocer demands his money, she hocks her Chinese chess set or just gives it to him.

This is her fourth or fifth trip to Paris. Only once did she come here with money in her pocket. Her custom is to arrive at a hotel, tell the *patron* to pay the taxi bill, engage a room and then borrow money from the *patron*. The next move is to the telegraph office. "Cable funds. Desperate. Ill." She has half a dozen stock forms which invariably bring results. Then she runs down to the Dôme, orders a chartreuse, and Montparnasse rubs its eyes. The curtain goes up. June loves her audiences.

They stare at her. They wonder about her cat's eye earrings which she never wears more than one at a time. Her lip rouge varies from all shades of red to green. Sometimes black. Her hats! There is one, à la Watteau, backed with a tuft of flowers, which she sports with a velvet cape and shantung dress. There is something inconsistent about a velvet cape, shantung dress and no stockings. And her face—her face looks like the patina of some old coin, marked with eyelashes of midnight blue.

"How do you judge me?" asked June, indifferently.

I hesitated. "Too much thyroid."

This led to another argument. After about another hour the concierge pounded on the door and said we were making too much noise.

*

1. Nikolai Stavrogin is the central character in Feodor Dostoevski's *The Possessed* (1872). June Mansfield apparently was not associated with the Provincetown Players. In 1924 she was, briefly, an understudy in the Theatre Guild's production of *Saint Joan*. See Jay Martin, *Always Merry and Bright The Life of Henry Miller* (Santa Barbara: Capra Press, 1978; London: Sheldon Press, 1979), pp. 93–96. Mansfield was Henry Miller's wife.

Tuesday, 19 January 1932, p. 4.

What does the Left Bank think about?

The *avant-garde*, the poets, the hermits—what do they think about? Why do they forsake the ordinary? It's the inner eye.

The inner eye goads them on; it forces their dreams with promises of extra-terrestrial booty. It makes victims of the guys on the Left Bank. New ideas are the coin of the Quarter, bright tokens beyond value. Bob Brown has a new idea. He played with it for 15 years, and now it pops without ceremony.

Bob offers the world a reading machine. It functions like a Wall Street ticker: words are to be printed in microscopic type on a winding spool of tape and read under a strong glass. Books will no longer be necessary, and 100,000 words may be concealed in a hollow tooth. Bob hopes by this process to speed up reading. If only he could speed up the human brain, the machine would be a wow, but it is not that modern.

This vague description is necessary for what follows. A "Readie" anthology has just been brought out with material specially adapted to the ma-

89

chine. "Unnecessary words" are deleted and punctuation has been re-formed to suit the instrument. The following extracts from the anthology will help explain the machine and the latest quiverings of the *avant-garde*. Limitations of ordinary newspaper type have made necessary a slight modification in the connecting signs. Further comment is superfluous.

Gertrude Stein: "We Came": "Prefers days to more-History must again be-Caught and taught and-Does who comes and-To play with balls-Few who are important-Nasturtiums than for."

Laurence Vail: "Boom the Doom": "NULLO-HOLE flat everest with flat iron of NULL and NO-with sponge o'NOTHING AT ALL."

George Kent: "I Think": "night is the business of getting the sun button . . . this button of sun . . . the son of a gun button . . . into the button-hole of dawn . . . button sighs daily I."

Nancy Cunard: "Dlink": "Poem plenny dreg-leg cork hat Middle ME (poem) dark stuff Flash-gold verdigrease . . . M. O. P. letter-love . . ."

Filippo Tommaso Marinetti: "Words in Freedom": "First Piston of Joy warm PENETRATE into the oil to fry wry frywry its nostalgia faaat faaat faat."

Norman Macleod: "Revelation": "romance-toreva-province-tusayan-moki deathofgod."

Sidney Hunt: "Morninight Car": "a bruPtinyjerk jerksfoot******BblLE EeCcHh O O O O O."

I think that's about enough. Oh, yes. The shortest offering—and some consider it the best while others consider it Alfred Kreymborg's best—goes as follows:

> Old man Kreymborg has grown too seedy
> To write Bob Brown a speedy readie.

The best explanation for all the material cited above was given by Lincoln Gillespie. Quoting from "Readievices": "sash & wile . . . booze . . . araminta‡ poothtaste err-er-er . . . aheheeholh‡ ditto‡ WOP . . . dental."[1]

They are glad to hear that Jimmie, the familiar Trojan, is back in the role of barman. Jimmie shakes cocktails with an aplomb and personal touch so satisfying to his customers, and for nine years the shifting groups have followed him. Now they are following him to his new spot, Romano's, off the Boulevard Raspail. Jimmie drinks tea.

Bill Seabrook and Marjorie Worthington will fly together tomorrow morning. They are bound for Timbuctoo, where 80 Whites spend their days in watching 50,000 natives beat their tom-toms. Bill and Marjorie are making this dark journey to whip into shape the life story of Père Yakouba, a Frenchman who found Paradise a generation ago. The mission, then, is literary, and Bill promised not to sample any more human flesh.[2] The authors should be back in about a month.

June Mansfield, the girl with the golden face, is returning to New York. Over the blend of six shades of powder she paints futuristic designs on her face. Thus Montparnassed, June will pursue a movie contract. Broadway will be up on its toes. Broadway will take one look and flit to Surrealism. It may welcome the new idea.

A protest!

Abraham Walkowitz is aroused because his work was not accepted for the American show which opened yesterday at the Galerie de la Renaissance.

"I am *the* American painter," he said.

"Perhaps you are," was the reply. "Consult the inner eye."

*

1. Bald quotes the following, not always accurately, from *Readies for Bob Brown's Machine* (Cagnes-sur-Mer: Roving Eye Press, 1931): Gertrude Stein, "We Came," pp. 100–101; Laurence Vail, "Boom the Doom," p. 15; George Kent, "Re. . . . Readies . . . I Think. . . . ," p. 75; Nancy Cunard, "Dlink," p. 124; Filippo Tommaso Marinetti, "Words in Freedom" (the second part of "Lyric Machine"), p. 47; Norman Macleod, "Ready: Revelation," p. 53; Sidney Hunt, "Morninight Car," pp. 150–51; Alfred Kreymborg, "Regrets," p. 114; A. Lincoln Gillespie, Jr., "Readievices," p. 91.
2. William B. Seabrook writes about Père Yakouba in *Jungle Ways* (1931) and *The White Monk of Timbuctoo* (New York: Harcourt, Brace, 1934; London: Harrap, 1934). He writes about his trip with Marjorie Worthington to interview Yakouba in *Air Adventure* (New York: Harcourt, Brace, 1933; London: Harrap, 1933). See p. 81, n. 3, n. 4.

Tuesday, 26 January 1932, p. 4.

Art is always interesting. The vernissage of the American show at the Galerie de la Renaissance was interesting. It had an emotional value.

I was particularly interested in the comments of the crowd. Kindly people drifted up to anxious artists and told them not to worry. That is the custom at vernissages. I was surprised to overhear a famous European sculptor remark that French art was well represented at the American show, even though the vitality was missing.

A near-sighted Frenchman stopped dead before the canvas of one of the exhibitors. "My God!" he exclaimed. "What's Soutine doing here?" The American turned white. There is always good drama at a vernissage. There was very good drama when Sam Ostrowski pushed Chil Aronson, the organizer, into a corner and made a pass at him. Even though the pass was intercepted, the story was good; but I kept it out of last Tuesday's column for sentimental reasons. Here at last was a good American show. That was the idea.

Tuesday, the next day, I met Ostrowski at the Dôme. He wasn't hung well. There was a plot somewhere. Politics, favoritism, Aronson was a double-crosser, he said. Then in walked Aronson, cadaverous, lusterless, neurotic. This show has made him and I think he deserves it; he has been kicked hard enough even while he was starving. I don't think he has the wit for intrigue. Luckily, I caught Ostrowski's wrist in time and pushed Aronson away. Aronson hurried away with the alacrity of a faun.

"They ought to shine my shoes and call me master!" shouted Abraham Walkowitz, another good American. "Aronson gives me the creeps." He wasn't admitted to the show. That is no count against him. Aronson is running the show and chose his heart's desires. Another 45 Americans might run a counter show, and I suspect that the quality would not be inferior.

Trouble had been brewing for at least a month before the vernissage. Art is an irritating disease, anyway. There were reports; there were rumors. Where was the joker in the deck? We'll come to that in a minute. Don't rush me. At 7 o'clock Friday night, Ary Stillman and Joseph Stella cracked each other with walking sticks. The battle of the artists. Stella was not in the show; Stillman was. Another Dôme brawl. The crowds gather, the cops laugh and the garçons serve more beer.

Such brawls are old stuff in the annals of Montparnasse. They are older than the decaying clichés of art critics. They are older than Henri Murger's slosh in his *La Vie de Bohème*.[1] But we long for something new, like American artists battling for a principle, not for the way they hang at an exhibit. Some day we'll get ambitious and fondle that theme with more precision.

Several of the boys are not contented. They weren't hung well—there was a dark reason. Jerry Blum is sore. Jerry is a member of the Government School of Beaux-Arts. To avoid misunderstanding, I am quoting him *verbatim*:

> The whole thing is a sell-out. It is dominated by Paul Burlin, who got the best wall and ran the show to suit himself. Why did Paul Burlin supply, through a friend of his, the deficit of 2,500 francs when it was previously agreed to split any deficit among the exhibitors?

Others deny this charge with vigor. Carl Holty, one of the outstanding abstract painters, insists that no such agreement had been made and that Burlin's only motive was to save the show by raising the needed sum. What's more, he added, some of the exhibitors were scratching pretty hard even to pay the fee.

There may be more battles, but I don't think anyone is going to get bumped off. They are all stars at the American show, each artist naturally absorbed in his own star. The whole business is a disgrace to the battered name of American endeavor. It must have provided the French with a good laugh.

Jean Cocteau provides new meat for Dôme chatter.

They are talking about his *avant-garde* movie, *The Blood of a Poet*, now running at the Vieux-Colombier.[2] It is a picture that attempts to employ the disorder of the subconscious, and a visit to the theatre may acquaint the reader with certain literary tendencies on the Left Bank. It reveals the same eczema.

But Cocteau doesn't imitate very well the bolder and more ingenious champions, Buñuel and Cavalcanti. Despite its careful symbolism (snow for cocaine, the applauding of death for sadism, etc.) the picture is as false as a gold tooth and just as obvious. Cocteau must be getting old, for he had to pluck the heart out of *Les Enfants Terribles* for its kernel.[3]

I was discussing the thing with Erskine Gwynne, cheery editor of *The*

Boulevardier, a stimulating monthly rag that appeals to so many Americans.[4] Gwynne thought that Alice in Wonderland came first, although Alice never resorted to opium. It reminded him, he added, of the night he went out with Venus and she came home with both her arms cut off. "Her mother was furious and blamed it on me." He was speaking parabolically.

We have just read his complete version in *The Boulevardier.* What does he think of Cocteau's film and other performances that mock lucidity? The cafés are buzzing again. What did Erskine Gwynne say in the current *Boulevardier?*

*
* *

1. Henri Murger (1822–1861) wrote about Bohemian life in "Scènes de la vie de Bohème" in *Corsaire* (1847–1849). *La Vie de Bohème* (1849) dramatizes his writings.
2. Jean Cocteau's *Le Sang d'un poète* was released in 1932.
3. Cocteau, *Les Enfants terribles* (Paris: Grasset, 1925); *Enfants terribles* (New York: Brewer & Warren, 1930).
4. Erskine Gwynne published every number of the *Boulevardier,* from March 1927 to, apparently, February 1933. Arthur Moss edited most of the numbers. A column entitled "The Left-Over Bank" was a regular feature beginning in April 1929. Of the writers of this column, Bald was the only one to use his real name.

Tuesday, 9 February 1932, p. 4.

I remember the time Louise Bryant gave a trunk to a couple of her cronies. She was always giving things away. They needed a trunk—she gave it to them.

It was heavy. The two inseparables, Mergault and Petroff, hoisted it to their shoulders and began the three block march to their studio. They were so drunk they couldn't stagger ten paces without dropping their burden, and when they reached the Boulevard du Montparnasse they deposited this trunk in the middle of the street and sat on it. Then they reached in their coat pockets for red wine and poured it down their throats.

The middle of the street is not a café. They were risking their lives, and taxi drivers yelled bitterly at the drunkards. The two Bohemians got sore and smashed their bottles on the highway. Their next move was to rush to either side of the street and wave their arms to stop all traffic. "Detour to save your tires!" yelled Petroff. The sidewalks were lined with the laughing multitude. Another occurrence in Montparnasse.

Where were the cops all this time? They were approaching quite leisurely. They knew Petroff, the Russian painter, and Mergault, the French poet. They helped them shoulder their trunk again and said *"Bonsoir,"* while a garçon swept the glass off the street. Some day I expect to write an ode to French cops because I can't understand them. French cops make me think of Voltaire.

We could evoke other escapades of the inseparables, Petroff and Mergault, but *pourquoi?* They did all the things Bohemians are expected to do. They were generally drunk at noon and drunk at midnight. They either went without sleep for three nights or slept the clock around. Some people call that *esprit*.

They must have served in the Navy at one time or another, for they had the habit of wandering in the bars and shouting the word "mer" at the world repetitiously. This one-word dialogue always brought a laugh. Mergault never appeared in public without a huge, white flower in his lapel and one in his hand. Sometimes he would sport a horse-shoe of laurel on his head, like Nero.

Perhaps the line of descent was Villon to Verlaine to Mergault. He liked to recite his verse to strangers, his voice full of passion, his arms weaving gracefully over his head, and his hands clutching the air as if to catch the ankles of a Muse in flight. *"Mon cœur! Miserere!"* Frustration makes Bohemians. Mergault never published a line, but he enjoyed the second prize, the luxury of an emotional fixation.

His history is interesting. He was born of bourgeois parents in Nantes. They disowned him for marrying an English actress. He went into business. His wife died. He dropped business, dropped everything, and began to write poetry. The cops understood Mergault and let him alone.

I saw him sitting in one of the cafés a month ago. Petroff was in the hospital. Mergault was alone. His eyes were murky, his lips were blue and his cheeks were nearly pinned together. His cough was bad. But his hair was dyed purple—another challenge to nature. The garçons wanted to eject him, because his appearance wasn't good for business. The clients objected. He remained. His coughs were last salvos to the Muse who had let him down. His *esprit* had let him down. The dice of the gods were loaded against

Mergault. His cough gave one the creeps. His mother arrived in Paris last week to bury him. A poet passes.

Louise Bryant left for America a few months ago. The Quarter knew her as a writer, a poet and an artist. They also knew her as a generous woman. Her studio in the Rue d'Assas, with its candles, ikons, silken fans, bronze images, and canvases, was a day and night club for everybody. Otto Kahn would call. Konrad Bercovici would call. Hemingway would call. None of them could forget Jack Reed's wife. But she will never come back to Montparnasse. Word has just reached us that she died in New York.

They will all meet some day: Louise Bryant, Mergault, Pascin, Cheever Dunning—if there is a Valhalla. But the Countess, Homer Bevans and Flossie Martin are still creating their own Valhallas in other neighborhoods.

After a silence of about 18 months, Eugene Jolas brings back to life *transition*, an experimental magazine of interest to most Left Bankers. The revived publication will be called *transition* 1932 and will be published at The Hague. Once again we will be reading about dream fantasies, and James Joyce will go on with his interrupted "Work in Progress," a tome not entirely incomprehensible. Jolas calls the magazine "an experimental laboratory for Orphic creation."[1] Read the first number of the new Orpheus next Monday.

*

1. *Transition*, 21 (March 1932), includes a section entitled "Homage to James Joyce." Photographs of Joyce's "Work in Progress" and of his corrections follow p. 258. Eugene Jolas, in his preface, notes that *transition* "proposes to establish a mantic laboratory that will examine the new personality . . ." (p. [6]).

Tuesday, 23 February 1932, p. 4.

The last blow to Montparnasse is the departure of Harold Stearns. He went to California where the warm sun revives tired people. He was tired of the monotony of his role.

Harold was a cerebral solitary who lived pleasantly in a passive world, and he used to sit at the Select and dream of old episodes. Once there was great promise, but there is something epic about great resignation. The latter is an enticing achievement, and Harold will always be regarded as a legendary figure, a good compensation.

Before leaving, all his teeth were extracted, it having been discovered that bad teeth was the only thing wrong with him physically. It is hoped that this operation will radically alter his viewpoint and make him forget the appeal of great resignation. The deans of the Quarter have not lost faith in one of the most promising young men of America.

The passing of Harold Stearns from Montparnasse is pointed to as one more symptom of its end. But new blood continues to pour in. New faces brighten the streets.

*
* *

Tuesday, 1 March 1932, p. 4.

We don't know much about Soho beyond the fact that it is located in London. They have a place called the Fitzroy Tavern, which is said to correspond, roughly, to the Dôme. It is a good station for art talk and English ale.

At any rate, Nina Hamnett is there. Until a few years ago she presided on the terrace of the Dôme, and among her "callers" were figures such as Modigliani, Léger, Frank Harris, George Moore, Leo Stein, Booth Tarkington, et al. In those days they crowded around Nina's table, and ideas were lightly exchanged while Nina strummed her mandolin.

Now that she is bringing out a book of memoirs, we recall that former period. There was Lady Duff Twysden, now married to Clinton King in Texas. Flossie Martin, the queen of dynamos, the complete Bohemian, was a big drawing card. Now she is an ocean away. There were Isadora Duncan, Louise Bryant, Mary Butts, Anna Wickham—all very positive women. Anna Wickham, whose poetry is widely read in America, is living at present somewhere in London.[1] We remember the occasion, one bright morning, when Anna was irritated by some remark uttered by a young woman sitting at the next table. Anna got up and froze her with the following: "I hate blonde molls full of wind and mood."

Nina's book will be called *Laughing Torso*, published by Constable and Co. There is a torso of Nina at the Victoria and Albert Museum; H. G. Brzeska is the sculptor. The story goes that the chunk of marble was chipped off a tombstone.[2] London journalists, according to Nina, picked up the story and wrote that she and the sculptor "were in the habit of wandering around graveyards at midnight, borrowing tombstones." Some journalists have a great sense of exaggeration.

Soho must be a lively place, because the Countess is there. The Countess writes that living in England is very complicated. The very first night, she was so exuberant that she rushed up to a London bobbie.

"Take me," she said, dropping her arms around his neck. "O take me to a night club." A bit taken aback by this Montparnasse behaviour, the bobbie took her to a police station. The Countess shouted and sang for several hours, until someone brought her a pair of roller skates, whereupon she gave an exhibition. They let her go immediately after. "I was feeling drunk and incapable," the Countess P. S.'d.

She will probably build up Soho. Nothing escapes her. At the Fitzroy Tavern she meets Liam O'Flaherty, Rona Benzie, Thomas Burke, and warms them with her Bohemian rays. Why shouldn't this irrepressible woman whistle? Rodin was a great whistler. So was Rembrandt.

Peter Neagoe's book of short stories, *Storm*, is causing considerable comment in Montparnasse. His next book will be called *Peter, the Great*, a tale about a man seven feet high, with a strong back and simple mind.[3] Note Neagoe's army of words. It is not a large army, but each word is well disciplined and knows exactly what to do. Perhaps that accounts for the subtle lyricism of his prose. His sentences have a wonderful *esprit*. *Storm* is hot stuff.

1. Anna Wickham published several volumes of poetry, beginning with *The Contemplative Quarry* (London: Poetry Bookshop, 1915; New York: Harcourt, Brace, 1921).
2. Nina Hamnett, *Laughing Torso* (London: Constable, 1932; New York: Long & Smith, 1932). A photograph of Henri Gaudier-Brzeska's torso of Hamnett serves as the frontispiece to both editions. On pp. 39-40 Hamnett writes about the tombstone marble.

3. Peter Neagoe, *Storm* (Paris: New Review Press, 1932). Neagoe did not publish *Peter, the Great*.

Tuesday, 8 March 1932, p. 4.

One of the most significant members of the Left Bank colonies has gone back to America. His influence on their intellectual life will long be remembered, and artists as well as writers have him to thank for the release of new avenues of creative interest. Thanks to his encouragement and example, progress has been made.

His name is Lincoln Gillespie, author of "Amerikaka." It starts like this:

> ghoubrel
> i shing my ostracization
> come back!
> come back, I implore you
> no—stay away
> here
> i am ecstaticly.[1]

The sensitive reader will see rainbows filtering through each image in the above lines. They tell of Link's struggle—how he arrived in Montparnasse some years ago with only ten dollars and a copy of *Ulysses*, how he often appeared at the Dôme with a manuscript in one pocket and a bottle of seltzer in the other, and how he astonished strangers by squirting seltzer at them if they didn't like his poetry. Culturally, he was an incorrigible pilgrim, but he was always patient.

So he went to Cagnes. In that Left Bank outpost, he saw the boys and girls drooping on the sands of the Mediterranean, perishing from exhaustion. "Behold the sybarites!" said Gillespie. "They cannot reap because they can no longer sow." He counseled them to transfer their interests, and now the colony of Cagnes is what it is. He taught them the meaning of new words and the modern disguise of ideas.

"One new word is worth two ideas, and one idea is better than a blonde," was his amazing doctrine. So most of his followers took up painting.

We have on hand a letter from Link wherein he explains why he is returning to America. He writes that the country, in its present state, should be open to suggestion. He expects to subdue the gangsters with words. Here are some of the words: "thwarteco," "hyprobably," "intulib," "nickdicker," "abstractions." Perhaps he will succeed, for words generally guide the mob. The letter ends with "I shall be quite a force for Amerality, and I plan to efface the Amer scene (somewhat obly) with proper coopulation and sound the non-histrionic Egoism of Democits." The virgins of Cagnes are lighting candles for his success.

*
* *

1. See p. 25, n. 1. The lines Bald quotes are not from Lincoln Gillespie's "Amerikaka Ballet."

Tuesday, 15 March 1932, p. 4.

We are sorry to see that Adolf Dehn is going back to America. The passing of Adolf leaves one more hole in Montparnasse.

He is returning home to Minnesota where the sun shines on Lake Tetonka and the birds are in the meadow. Adolf will fish in the lake and shoot the birds on the trees, but he will never forget his devotion to the ultra-civilization of the Quarter. It's got him.

Living here a long time has given him a certain detachment, a quietus that nothing can disturb. People in the Quarter are in the habit of speaking of "Adolf's calm," as if they were discussing a cocktail party or Picasso. He is not even excited about leaving for America. Some of his friends have called him "Take-it-easy Adolf."

He will stop off at the Weyhe Gallery in New York to supervise an exhibit of his lithographs and caricatures there. We hear that his work has been compared to [that of] the German Grosz. But he lacks the latter's naked bitterness; in fact, his stuff on Harlem and night-club life that appears in *Vanity Fair* and *The New Yorker* tells a lot about his forgiving eye.[1]

And his sun-dodging habit. Adolf likes to prowl and work at night. Then, as the sky changes color, he greets the dawn with a little smile and walks from the Dôme to his roof-garden studio near the Eiffel Tower. After climbing the winding stairs, he fries a couple of eggs, does a lithograph and goes to sleep. That regime will be difficult in Minnesota.

*
* *

1. Adolf Dehn exhibited his work at the Weyhe Gallery, New York, in 1923, 1935, 1938, 1939, and 1940. For examples of his "Harlem and night-club life" scenes, see *Adolf Dehn Drawings* (Columbia: University of Missouri Press, 1971), pp. 44–61.

Tuesday, 22 March 1932, p. 4.

Transition has been revived and Eugene Jolas is back in Montparnasse.[1] Things are getting lively again.

During its three-year span, the magazine was recognized as representative of the Left Bank *mind*: I refer loosely to a reputation for progress, intellectual revolt and *avant-gardism*. Which explains, perhaps, the local interest in the first new number.

We find the same plea for new language, sublime chaos and the sovereignty of expression. The value of this approach cannot be overlooked, and young writers have been stimulated by generous examples. New words should be coined, for instance, for the sake of utility, but there is ever the danger that talent may be consumed in vain pursuit of that utility. Besides, it may make the reader self-conscious and the reading a bit rugged.

And yet no chronicler of life in Montparnasse can afford to overlook the beneficent influence of *transition*. One might compare it to *The New Review*, edited by Samuel Putnam. I think that if you compare the two magazines you are comparing the two editors, and further than that, you are contrasting two conflicting and yet complementary modes of thought in Montparnasse.

One is collective, the other is individual; one is logical, the other is intuitive; one is cold, the other is passionate; one is sane, the other is poetic. It is the old issue of content versus form. Further observations and manifestoes are unnecessary. You might add that both extremes are dangerous: sterility on the one hand and frenzy on the other. After all, too much clear thinking offers only lassitude, and poetry and madness live in the same basement.

Give us more Putnams and Jolases. Their influence on thought in this creative neighborhood has been considerable. They are both honest men, and I am convinced of their sincerity. Neither are [*sic*] smug; they are competent troubadours. They experiment differently because they are made differently. Their magazines are their outer garments and should set the fashion for other creators. Between these two forces, these two giants, lies piqued curiosity, and that's me.

*
* *

Wedding bells for Kay Boyle and Laurence Vail.

It will take place in Nice on April 2. After that, life in Villefranche will go on just the same. The couple have been close friends for a few years, and the Villefranche chateau is a favorite nook for the wandering writers and artists of the Riviera.

Both writers made their bow a few years ago in *transition*, mentioned above somewhere. Lately, Kay has been making rapid strides in the literary world, and *Plagued by the Nightingale*, I understand, made a big splash. Laurence has recently published his thoroughly modern novel, *Murder! Murder!* a work not at all sadistic.

We hear that among those present will be Peggy Guggenheim, Vail's first, but we haven't received word about the intentions of M. Brault, Kay's first, who lives in London.[2] Montparnasse is quite goggy about the coming event.

*
* *

1. Bald refers to *transition*, 21 (March 1932).
2. See pp. 86-87, n. 2, and p. 13, n. 1. In 1922 Laurence Vail married Peggy Guggenheim and Kay Boyle married Richard Brault. Vail and Boyle married in 1932; they were divorced in 1941.

Tuesday, 29 March 1932, p. 4.

*
* *

The social season over here was launched by Gwen Le Gallienne, a girl of such poise that when she enters a room she appears to be stepping down from a cloud.

Gwen threw a party in her father's studio in the Rue Servandoni, a strange attic surrounded by roof-tops and pigeons. The room was lit by long candles that threw a pale, timid light on the faces of generals, poets, barons, etchers, dancers, and a few of the herd.

Everyone thought it great fun when Gwen suddenly slipped behind a screen and then slipped back again in a Gandhi costume. Then, without warning or music, she leaped in the air with the grace of a doe and started to do the Phoebe dance, a difficult performance requiring great skill and agility. The dance was terminated when she accidentally stepped on Chang, her pet cat, who screeched with such abandon that the flickering candle lights were almost extinguished.

Life is more than play to Gwen. When in the mood she paints, and the weather being what it is, she does most of her painting on the perilous perch you may view on this page. To get there she has to climb two ladders, and she can see the city of Paris far below, but she is not afraid of plunging to the murky depths. Gwen, who is really a dreamer, says that that lofty stand is so much closer to the moon.

We hear that George Reavey will soon have his first book of poems ready. He says that *Faust's Metamorphoses* will be a little like Spengler and a lot like Marlowe.[1] That doesn't leave much room for George Reavey, but we shall see. Bill Hayter, whose exhibition of modern drawings is still running at the Galerie Vignon, will do the illustrations.

Bob Brown, the literary demon of Cagnes, whose anthology, *The Readies*, was discussed here a few Tuesdays ago, has just had his first novel accepted. *You Gotta Live* will be brought out by Harmsworth in the fall. The length alone should recommend it—130,000 words.

And his book, *Let There Be Beer*, is just finished. We understand that H. L. Mencken has bought several chapters for *The American Mercury*. How does Bob stand? Is he for or against Prohibition? The answer may be hidden in some of the abstruse passages of the *Readies*.[2]

*
* *

The art dealer Zborowski died last week to the regret of everyone who knew him, and there were many. He was a great friend of Soutine, and their tribulations in the early days are recalled.

One day Zborowski found Soutine in dire straits and went out to purchase food. Meanwhile Soutine had started a fire on which to cook it, and for fuel he used some of his canvases. Zborowski was horrified and put out the blaze, which was burning merrily.

The dealer once saw an exhibition of fake Soutines. He and the artist entered the luxurious boutique, and ended a long argument by thrusting their feet and walking sticks through the counterfeit pictures. The guilty party was one of Soutine's best friends who had often watched him work. Such incidents were lively.

That was the old Bohemia, the pre-jazz Montparnasse.

*

1. See p. 59, n. 1.
2. See p. 67, n. 1. Bob Brown, *You Gotta Live* (London: Harmsworth, 1932); *Let There Be Beer!* (New York: Smith & Haas, 1932). Excerpts from the latter book appear as "Pages from the Book of Beer," *American Mercury*, 26.102 (June 1932), pp. 185–91, and "Drug-Store in a Dry Town," *American Mercury*, 26.104 (August 1932), pp. 405–11.

Tuesday, 19 April 1932, p. 4.

Take a good look at literature in Montparnasse. *The New Review* has fallen for wine and women. *The New Review* has gone tabloid. Are there no more serious persons left?

In the current number, broken hearts are squealing. Listen to the cry of Laurence Vail, stifled, disillusioned and weary. After a pan-Proustian analysis of toxical jealousy, he exclaims: "Home. There's a hole there. It bleaks my plexus dreadful. My heart moons in a frigidaire. The cold hole gapes awful dismal. Awful if I roll insomniacly when I go to bed. Too awful."

Nancy Cunard does the Jean-Jacques Rousseau thing and tells all. David Martin strikes the proper young note of futility: "I am doing this and this. I am calm but I do not know what verbs or this and this are about." Kay Boyle writes "In Defense of Homosexuality," and in the opening line the poet makes a prophecy: "I speak of it as a thing with a future."

Ford Madox Ford describes himself from the very first sentence: "When I was a little, little boy and looked presumably like an angel Raphael. . . ." Now! In explaining Neagoe's story, *Storm*, Samuel Putnam reaches the heights of melodrama: "Go with the approaching terror in the darkly lowering STORM, a crackling terror, the crackling of a conflagration that approaches with wolf-step over the frozen snow. . . . strong male love. . . . twin patches of moonlight. . . . adolescent's bedroom floor. . . . Little Nell. . . ."[1]

This is Montparnasse. Will you step over to the next cage? Eugene Jolas has just brought out a pamphlet extension of *transition*, an experimental magazine recently revived. The pamphlet is called *The Language of Night*, in contrast to the language of early morning, referred to above.[2] Whereas the covers of *The New Review* are absinthe green, *The Language of Night* is bound in chthonian red.

Jolas warns the world of the metanthropological crisis. A crisis like that cannot hurt anybody, and Montparnasse prefers that one to any other. Montparnasse is rather advanced that way. Economics and politics will blunder to their crude solutions, but all that is cared about is the crisis of language and the revolution of the word. Literature he praised. Literary games can be played by anyone and there is no fatigue.

The doctrines in *The Language of Night* ask to be accepted on faith. I like to read what Jolas has to say, not for conviction but to bask in his exuberance. He insists upon mediumistic rhythms, alogical construction and mauling the alphabet. Perhaps literary progress lies that way. No one should demand reasons when he calls for the undermining of reason in language. To do so is absurd. I accept what he has to say. I mean I accept it as I accept any performance on the stage. It's interesting.

"Clipping the yet intact Ova between his rubbery helix and hypertrophied mastoid process. . . . let me off the tutti chords now and tell me frankly shutting your eyes like Rouletabille what you think of my erotic sostenutino. . . . his shingles and his graphospasms and his weeping eczema." This was taken and cut at random from the pages of *transition*.[3] Perhaps the author was joking. If not, it is safe to conclude that anyone who bites the English language like that must have tortured flies when he was very young. Yes, it's interesting.

1. *New Review*, 2.5 (April 1932), includes Laurence Vail's "Prettier and Prettier," pp. 79-83 (the quotation is from p. 81); Nancy Cunard's "Black Man and White Ladyship," pp. 30-35; David Martin's "A Heap of Jack Straws," pp. 27-29 (the quotation is from pp. 27-28); Kay Boyle's "In Defense of Homosexuality," pp. 24-25 (the quotation is from p. 24); Ford Madox Ford's "Pound and 'How to Read,' " pp. 39-45 (the quotation is from p. 39); Samuel Putnam's "The Preaching to the Fishes" (a review of Peter Neagoe's *Storm*), pp. 68-72 (the quotation is from pp. 68-69).
2. Eugene Jolas, *The Language of Night* (The Hague: Servire, 1932).
3. Source unknown.

Tuesday, 26 April 1932, p. 4.

Sinclair Lewis is all right. He is very thin and has red hair, but he is all right. Every time I asked him a question he jumped from his chair and laughed. The telephone rang and rang.

"Don't answer that phone," I cautioned him. "People chase the big shots. You're a pretty big shot. They want favors."

"Forget it," he said. "Before they open up I tell them 'I can't afford to do it' or something like 'The crisis has hit me too.' That's what I get for being a celebrity. Gosh, how I hate celebrities."

The telephone rang again. He picked up the receiver. "No!" he shouted and hung up. "Can you beat it?" he said to me. "More autograph hunters. They wake me up in the middle of the night."

I felt very sorry for him. "That Nobel Prize," I said, "is the cause of all this trouble. You're a marked man." The brandy was very good. We raised our glasses and had another drink. I was ready to roll on the floor. That's how sorry I felt for him.

Dorothy came in from the next room. She felt sorry for him, too. "All day long," she said, "people have been pursuing him. I have just arrived and can't get a minute alone with him." She has her troubles. Dorothy wrote *I Saw Hitler*, and a couple of journalists had been waylaying her in the next room.[1] Through the oaken panel I had heard them shouting "What about Germany?" and "When will your big stories appear in the *Saturday Evening Post?*"

"Tell me that one about Hugh Walpole again," I was addressing Sinclair, "and make it snappy before that telephone rings again." I asked him to tell it in English this time. He has a habit of breaking out in violent German. "Ach ja!" What a hit Sinclair Lewis would have been on the vaudeville stage!

"Well, one day a girl reporter was sent to interview Walpole, after one of his lectures. You know the kind—68 and pleasant (he mimicked her lisp)— and Walpole was tired. So I said to the reporter 'I will interview Walpole and he will interview me. Then you'll have a swell story.' "

"So what?" said I, the anxious questioner.

"So she turned to me and said quite tartly, 'I beg your pardon, sir, but I was not instructed to interview *you*.' "

"Ho ho," I remarked, rolling on the floor. I almost rolled out of the window. "Ho ho." Then I rose to my knees.

"Give me your slant on Montparnasse and tell me about Ann Vickers."

The telephone rang again. "It's Gilbert White and Jimmy Donohue," said the wiry redhead. "What shall I do?"

"Let them come up," I instructed. "After all, Gilbert is an old friend of yours. They'll want you to speak before the American Club."

His face sank in despair. "I won't. Hello! Come up."

Gilbert and Jimmy came up and we had another round of brandy. Then Gilbert opened up.

"Come on, Red," he said coaxingly. "We've got you. You are going to give us a nice talk at the American Club next Thursday. We're counting on you." Gilbert adjusted his monocle to aid conviction.

Red sighed firmly. "Not a chance," he said. "I will not speak before the American Club."

High-pressure salesmanship was necessary. "Come on," said Jimmy, "we promised that you would talk."

"And," said Gilbert, following up, "you should uplift your fellow Babbitts. Don't be a prima donna. Look at me. I always speak, and it keeps me awake and everything." With all this arguing going on, a swell chance I had getting a slant on Montparnasse. Incidentally, there aren't many more slants on Montparnasse. All that was accomplished ten years ago.

So they argued and argued, and the telephone kept ringing. We called the garçon for more brandy. We called him several times. Red absolutely refused to speak before the American Club. At times, he reinforced his refusal with more brandy and outbursts of German. He can even swear in German. At last, the other guests left. I felt very sorry for him. He looked very tired. Dorothy was very tired. I was very tired. The Nobel Prize is only a succubus. The Nobel Prize is worse than a beautiful mistress. But it does satisfy. It looks good.

1. Dorothy Thompson, *"I Saw Hitler!"* (New York: Farrar & Rinehart, 1932).

Tuesday, 14 June 1932, p. 4.

Only the higher problems affect George Reavey; the ordinary perplexities mean nothing to him. He is haunted by the absolute.

Reavey thinks in terms of new values; his pale face covers a brilliant chaos, and his ideas charge madly towards solution. His demeanor is calm and pleasant, but his interior throbs with despair. His spiritual tangle is interesting, for there must be a certain joy in weighing the universe.

We are considering a young Irish poet who lives in Montparnasse. He is small, saintly-looking, and he speaks slowly and distinctly over a red beard. I once asked him to explain the genesis of his chin weeds.

"I had decided to let my beard grow," he replied, "until one of my long poems reached the end. But after it was finished I looked in the mirror. So I kept the beard and tore up the poem." Explanations by poets are always interesting.

"What haunts you most?" I asked.

"The architectural symbolism of the age is highly significant to me," he said. "I have been pondering over the new values, but thus far I haven't been able to do anything about it."

Reavey was wrong. He has done something about it; he is responsible for *Faust's Metamorphoses*, his first book of poems, just brought out. The volume explains his sense of calamity: "I am the restless urge, the widowed, destined soul."[1] In the book he unlocks the doors of his metaphysical grief. It's all about his swooning resolutions.

To write the book Reavey sought retirement in a Montparnasse studio. There he lived like a monk and practised abstention. To punish his material self he would sleep on the floor and sing hymns in the morning. In the beginning he sang them at night but almost got arrested, so he changed his singing schedule.

"Did you wear sackcloth underwear?" I asked.

"I didn't wear any underwear," he said. "My spirit didn't need any underwear."

And so his poems were bred in seclusion, and his rigorous meditation has advanced his clarity. Quoting from his book in which he explains his position:

> Volutes of molumn whorl
>   towards daos
> Abracadabr(a) is
>   mnemonic lozenge
> to thy foal's limple doubt
>   song unrevolved.[2]

The quoted lines taken from "To Icarus" clarify the ache of the actual while disregarding the cosmic chill. They also prove that the soul is elastic. Personally, I think the soul is too tolerant to poets, but that doesn't concern us now.

In the latter days of the Roman Empire people fed up with society fled to the desert where they lived without interference. Now the deserts are too far away and not conveniently reached, so the hermit must retire within himself. There is no desert like one's own. Reavey is now loose in the cafés of Montparnasse, and his next retirement is scheduled for next fall. A second volume of poetry will probably escape.[3] This duality is one explanation of *Faust's Metamorphoses*.

For Reavey bears a wound. He is exalted by misfortune and feels himself stronger with each blow.

"How do you explain your power of resistance?" I asked.

"My sense of predestination," was his comeback. Which doesn't explain hard blows like:

> Then in a blackwinged whir she fled
> And left me pondering on the edge.[4]

The above is one instance where the ideal turns its face away at the crucial moment. To him, apparently, the significance of woman dissolves at the wrong time. *C'est triste, mon vieux.* Reavey is bothered by the recurrence of death and tragic love. He throws bombs at our age, and they explode in his own startling visions. Knowing his Dante, he says that woman was a proper intermediary between man and the universe, that she was the coordinate symbol of love. But woman can no longer attain this unity. I have always suspected our flappers.

But read his poetry and note the variety of forms; each poem finds a form from simple statement to what is considered purely lyrical: a minute metamorphosis springs from each form. The Faust mind wavers between classical meter and shrewd play of words. But Reavey has a tendency to summarize at the end of each poem. Why must poets summarize? Why do they vulgarize their precious chaos?

They all struggle towards light. Painters have been struggling towards light too long, according to Man Ray, the pioneer camera man who gave up painting about 12 years ago.

"Painting," he says, "dates back 5,000 years and photography only 50. Photography is the future of art."

Man Ray has concluded his experiments on "solarization," a camera-less secret for the control of a powerful outline around the object. He will show the results at the international exposition at Brussels next month.[5]

*
* *

1. George Reavey, "Faust's Reincarnation by the Good Angel," *Faust's Metamorphoses* (Fontenay-Aux Roses: New Review Editions, 1932), p. 60.
2. Reavey, "To Icarus," *Faust's Metamorphoses*, p. 49.
3. Reavey's next volume of verse was *Nostradam* (Paris: Europa Press, 1935).
4. Reavey, "Metamorphosis of Love," *Faust's Metamorphoses*, p. 57.
5. Man Ray participated in the "Exposition internationale de la photographie" (Palais des Beaux-Arts, Brussels) in 1932.

Tuesday, 12 July 1932, p. 4.

CAGNES-SUR-MER (By Mail.)—

*
* *

Lincoln Gillespie, medicine man of Cagnes, writes from Philadelphia that he is considering a cultural promotion for America. He intends to open up a chain of jazz salons where he will encourage discussions on every conceivable prophecy. Link writes: "As for myself, I hope to lecture on Pizzikaks and volotonous porispils. There is something loose in the Ameribund ridicachase."

The lecturer also hopes to invent several new languages. People still contend that he owes his facility to long exposure in the Montparnasse social stream. In America he may recover gradually. Gillespie also denies that he is engaged to Peggy Joyce. Someone in Cagnes must have started that rumor.

There is a small serious group headed by Ross Saunders, the Surrealist painter recently elected Mayor of the American colony. Ross is also an engineer and was loudly cheered when he tried to perfect Bob Brown's perpetual reading machine.

*
* *

George Antheil, the hard-working composer, is back from a visit to Berlin after spending a year in America.

His next opera, written in collaboration with John Erskine, will be produced in America and Germany next year. It's called *Helen Retires*, revolving about the resurrected Helen's last adventure.

"My opera," said George, "may prove that love is not operatic. The old formulas are done away with."

"What's it about?"

"Helen is pretty old and ready to die. She wants one more grand affair, so she goes to hell, searching for Achilles. But he's only a ghost and not very useful, and she dismisses him. After she returns to earth she discovers that an ordinary fisherman is studying her with interest. She asks the fisherman what he wants. 'Helen,' he replies. The heroine powders her nose, looks at her mirror and melts for the plebian."

That's how our modern age regards the face that launched a thousand ships.

Nancy Cunard, according to Antheil, is still adventuring in America. Her Negro anthology, which she has been threatening to bring out the past two years, will comprise 2,000 pages. Antheil has collected the music.[1]

*
* *

1. George Antheil contributed "The Negro on the Spiral or a Method of Negro Music" to Nancy Cunard's *Negro Anthology* (London: Nancy Cunard at Wishart, 1934), pp. 346–51. "Congo Songs Bacongo Tribe," Antheil's music, appears on pp. 419–20.

Tuesday, 16 August 1932, p. 4.

Once, while eating macaroni at Rosalie's, a party of three women and their boy friends were acting very American.

Not knowing Rosalie they rapped sharply for better service, and the other clients heard their chirps of irritation with something bordering on alarm.

They were going to get it!

Then she emerged from the kitchen, this old woman wrapped in a shawl, her feet encased in carpet slippers and her great black eyes alive as an outraged Fortuna's. The offenders cringed before the approaching Sibyl; their foregone assurance melted like ice cream.

"Get out!" said Rosalie. Her voice was as steady as a torch. "I don't want the bourgeois here. Let your servants wait on you."

The six beans on vacation were utterly flattened, and their apologies spurted for several minutes.

"We're so sorry!"

The other clients tittered. Most of them had had their lesson. I had had mine. Rosalie was too genuine ever to be trifled with.

Her sturdy Roman face then relaxed and beamed so compellingly that everyone in the place breathed easier and smiled across the tables. The storm had passed. She embraced, metaphorically, the delinquents, and before leaving they smothered her with effusions.

That was Rosalie.[1]

She's gone now. Rosalie leaves Montparnasse.

Traditions are but tardy promises of contiguity. Another prop falls, but Montparnasse is still a name. The shrieks of Bohemians become rocking-chair songs, and the Old Guard smoke their pipes in the shadows of the Dôme. Art is as good an irritant as any, and the feeling is persistent. Montparnasse may grow broad and careless, but the Old Guard doesn't care. Ask Shorty Lasar, Alex Altenburg, the Warshawsky brothers, Kathleen O'Connor, Howell Cresswell, Major Helwig or Pop Eaton. They all knew Rosalie back in the old days. All of this, dear reader, (*sotto voce*) was long before my time.

The passing of Rosalie recalls so many legends I don't know where to begin. I have a dinner date in ten minutes, anyway. Her little place on the Rue Campagne-Première was a landmark: it nourished hungry artists, some of whom have bounced to glory in the last few years.

Rosalie was wise, for she had heard the secret ululations of the lost gentry, that band of earth forsakers who crept through mud to watch the sun. She tapped their insulation and understood the cravings of art's suberose troglodytes, many of whom should have been peddling neckties or locomotives.

Art is man's most profound conceit and measures, after its fashion, rotten mortal intrigues. I should think that Prometheus, if ever he had any brains, would easily understand, and then turn over and lay an egg. Montparnasse is a dying ambition.

The fact that Rosalie was once Whistler's model is merely an incident. Ask Picasso about her. Ask Utrillo, Kisling, Guerin, or Matisse.

Modigliani was her favorite. He would come into her little restaurant so drunk that he slept on her kitchen floor two to three days on end. Modigliani, whom the critics accepted after he was beaten into a corpse by poverty, was understood by a few women, one of whom leaped to death from a window the day he was buried. Then the critics were ignited and acclaimed Modigliani.

What could be more fetching of romance than the picture of a group of artists sketching by candle light from midnight till dawn? Modigliani and his friends would use Rosalie's premises for this slavish zeal. Some of the sketches were sold for 50 centimes; the others were deposited in Rosalie's basement only to be enjoyed by rats.

The legends pass with Rosalie, and the new Montparnasse spawns as ever. Ten years from now? The worm can't die.

Down in Majorca, Mary Dahlberg lives in the chateau where once George Sand and Chopin throbbed. The present mistress wrote *Dagger* and *Cocktail Cavalcade*.[2]

"At night," writes Mary, "the spirit of Chopin, or rather, his music, haunts the place. Here there is the torture of doubt and *mañana, mañana*."

Deep in the wilds of Majorca, Mary is fashionable and wears a diamond brooch so solid that not even a bullet can effect a penetration. One day, while awaiting her *couturière*, she was resting in equivocal *negligée* on a couch.

In walked Whit Burnett by accident.

Mary didn't know him, and her voice was soft. "Now you may measure me," she declared, in a grand fashion, and stared at the ceiling.

Whit's blonde goatee fluttered, and he hurried, perplexed, home again.

*
* *

1. Rosalie's surname was Tabia.
2. Mary Dahlberg's only book is *Dagger* (New York: Duffield, 1930).

Tuesday, 6 September 1932, p. 4.

*
* *

We hear that Jean Cocteau will come over from Saint-Mandrier. He expects to be in at the première of Edouard Bourdet's new play.[1]

It would be interesting if the nimble scribe would consent to appear before the Dôme in his southern outfit. Down in Saint-Mandrier Spotlight Jean dresses like a Turkish dancer. His flappy silk pantaloons are tucked in short Russian boots and his dappled jacket is distinguished with a green and purple motif. A great red scarf balances his vertical black hair. Evidently, the celebrity is taking no chances.

Back to the Quarter comes Dick Thoma, after a short holiday. The poet, lecturer and general esthete is working on *The Promised Land*, which he hopes to finish soon.

The first part, "Corpses in Sunlight" (quotation from Seabrook), concerns itself with a new theme: What about the spiritual existence?[2] Dick hopes to develop the idea for all it's worth. "People," he once told his friends, "should lead a spiritual life."

The theme ends in an attenuated wish. After many trials the hero's heart goes winging up to the stars as the body (Plato's shell) drops to the cold earth from one of the branches of a hickory tree. There it lies, utterly neglected, while the spirit, seated on a horn of Jupiter, indulges in glucose meditation. And that is why salvation drips from the Image.

*
* *

One or two letters have come in, asking an explanation of last Tuesday's note that Aldous Huxley has taken to painting.

The implication was that Huxley is interested in painting only as a hobby. The literary work goes on, for better or worse. In fact, he has just finished writing an introduction to *Letters of D. H. Lawrence*.[3]

Huxley's new pet is characteristic of the man. One may almost venture the statement that he is interested in everything. He is one of the most mentally active persons I have ever come across, and conversation with him is an excursion through every conceivable field of fortified data, with Huxley, of course, leading the way. It may begin with Bach's fugues and end with Russian politics.

His occasional appearance at the Dôme always brings a stare. He is almost six and one half feet of angles, measuring from his large black hat to the floor. Although only 38 he looks like a person who has been concentrating for 75 years. Maria is generally taking books out of his pocket because he reads too much.[4] He wears very thick glasses, and he gives the impression of being very shy and not quite aware of anyone, not even himself. He is very modest.

To conclude the digression, one afternoon last year Huxley was leaning against the old zinc bar with a leaf of poems in his hand.

A local poet wanted his opinion. So absorbed was he that, in a clear and enthusiastic voice, he began to read aloud, dramatic pauses and everything. The milling crowd stopped their clamoring, something like a hush unfolded and even the garçons looked up. At last he handed them back. From his great height he smiled patiently at the poet. "They are very, very bad," he said slowly. Then he walked away.

*
* *

1. Edouard Bourdet's *La Fleur des pois* opened in Paris on 4 October 1932.
2. Richard Thoma, *The Promised Land* (Paris: Nine rue Vavin, 1935?). In William B. Seabrook's *The Magic Island* (New York: Harcourt, Brace, 1929), the illustration facing p. 98 has this caption: "No one dared to stop them, for they were corpses walking in the sunlight." The sentence is in Seabrook's text, p. 99.
3. In his column of 30 August 1932, Bald notes that "Aldous Huxley, in Toulon, has taken up painting." Huxley edited *The Letters of D. H. Lawrence* (New York: Viking, 1932; London: Heinemann, 1932).
4. Maria Nys was Huxley's wife.

Tuesday, 27 September 1932, p. 4.

Once I visited Hilaire Hiler in his studio on the Rue Broca. We talked about painting.

Placed about the large room were 20 or 30 canvases—several were monumental in size and all of them betrayed a purpose, a method that indicated a rational program on the part of the artist.

Hiler had a theory.

He spoke of mathematical composition, the geometrical instinct, the scientific use of color. He said that before using color he carefully prepared a plan; then he executed it with the punctiliousness of a scientist.

Where is the line between art and science?

I sat back, smoking a *bleu,* and watched him work. He employs all the instruments of a mechanical drawing set: the ruler, the triangle, the compass, the stencil. Hiler works like an architect.

A few weeks after, I returned to his studio. Color had been applied so shrewdly on the canvas that the mechanical skeleton had taken on flesh. The problems of space had been met by color harmonies. I smoked another cigarette.

He was opposed to abstract painting because it ignored associative psychological elements; he was opposed to representational painting because it ignored physiological factors and because it was a recognized bore. He wouldn't compromise.

"A painting must satisfy man's geometrical instinct."

The reader may form his own opinion. Obviously, a discussion of the "geometrical instinct" has no place in this strip. The subject is presented at length and in its simplest terms because your correspondent considers it an American movement born in Montparnasse.

Within the last three years Neonaturism (as Hiler calls it) has spread over the coteries of French painters. French schools calling themselves *"neonaturalistes"* acknowledge the American preceptor. The term explains itself: the artist employs (disciplines) nature by selecting recognizable objects to fit a preconceived pattern. This pattern is shed by the subconscious but developed by the conscious, the latter deliberately using the recipes of modern art.

Reduced to a clause, Neonaturism is the submission of nature to the laws of abstract painting.

*
* *

Nina Hamnett, once a belle of Montparnasse, retired to England and wrote a book about it. Her revelations, *Laughing Torso,* was [sic] another one of those flamingo biographies.[1]

She wrote something about Aleister Crowley. He didn't like it and is suing her. Aleister Crowley was shocked.

That brings back old memories. Crowley is author of *The Diary of a Drug Fiend,* and he knew all about alchemy.[2] The only vegetation on his shaved head was a saffron forelock, called "Cling-Clong." He went in for green lights and incantations. He gave grand rocking-parties, and he spoke of Black Magic and hypnotism as one speaks of the stock market—always with an air of uncertainty. He was a character of Montparnasse. He is the hero of many legends. Stories about him would fill a waste basket.

Crowley is also a lecturer in London. Last week he spoke at one of Foyle's literary luncheons at the Grosvenor House on the philosophy of magic (Magick).

He became famous a few years ago when he invented the Kubla Khan No. 2 cocktail. Now he is suing Nina.

Here is an extract from the book:

Nina visited Crowley's studio. He greeted her, walked away calmly and immediately fell asleep. "He was lying on the hearthrug in front of the fire asleep. He woke up, stared at me and said, 'Are you alone?' I said 'Yes,' and he lay down and went to sleep again."[3]

Perhaps Nina should sue Crowley.

Jimmie, the barman, is back from a long vacation at Gre-sur-Loire [*sic*]. He says that Eric and Peggy Scott would watch him spar with Marion Rites, an artist who will give a show here soon. Jimmie says everyone had a good time and romped about in knickers. The Duc de Cardon acted as referee.

*
* *

1. See pp. 98-99, n. 2.
2. See p. 33, n. 2.
3. The quotation is from Nina Hamnett's *Laughing Torso,* p. 31.

Tuesday, 18 October 1932, p. 4.

One hundred years from now, professors will be lecturing on Montparnasse: its development and decay.

I feel safe in making that prediction because there is no fear of contradiction. There is something sublime about phrases like "The Decline of the

Roman Empire" or "The Last Days of Pompeii" or "The Glory That Was Greece" or "What Was the Matter with Montparnasse?"

Custodians like Plutarch, Herodotus and myself accept our mission with vision and humility. The world needs a lot of reporters; otherwise, it might get lost and disappear on the other side of Jupiter. A reporter is a man who follows news and thinks he's leading it. I once knew a girl who had a society job on a paper. "Without me and the publicity," she said, "there would be no society. The old ladies would stop giving parties."

Montparnasse, unlike Gaul, is divided into two parts: one is called Montparnasse and the other is the St. Germain district. The St. Germain district, a long walk from the Dôme, is commonly defined as the Deux Magots, Lipp's or Flore's.

This division of Apollo's Hangout is as destructive as a civil war. We cannot have solidarity so long as poets and translators desert the Dôme and plant themselves in the St. Germain district, where the boys and girls sit with folded hands and imagine they have outgrown something.

Last Friday night, at Lipp's, a party of Americans were asked to leave because one of the girls spoke above a whisper. They filed out, but did they hurry back to the Dôme? No, they went across the street to Flore's. That's where reformed Bohemians go now.

As a final argument I offer the testimony of Reynolds Packard, a poet of notorious promise: "I am so fed up with café restrictions around the St. Germain carrefour that I intend to hurry to Indo-China, where a man can eat any way he likes. The other night I was thrown out of the brasserie across the street because I dipped my oysters in the sauce instead of pouring the sauce over the oysters. They threw me out for that, mind you. They want to dominate us Americans."

"Oh, that's nothing," said Mary Cahill, who had been making eyes all evening. "They once threw me out because I laughed at a bald-headed waiter. He had three thin strings of hair brushed back over his head, and I told him he looked like a harp."

*
* *

Tuesday, 22 November 1932, p. 4.

Take a banker and a bum. Add an artist or a Russian spy. They're all the same to Louise Bryant.

From the four corners of this ball of dirt they have been calling on her for years. Sometimes they would call about 4 o'clock in the morning, waking up the concierge, but rarely disturbing the nuns sleeping in their cells across the garden. For Louise lives in a cloister on the Rue d'Assas.

A night-owl myself, I have often called on her after leaving the Dôme long after midnight, only to find, on occasion, men and women regarded by journalists as front page stuff. Possibly in one corner of the huge cell would be discovered a couple of starving poets who had no other place to sleep.

So you'll grant me the liberty, then, of calling her the hostess of Montparnasse. What do all these people want? Just a little sustenance—a handout for an artist; the celebrities ask the solace of unadorned conversation.

I remember the time Bercovici, fretful and worried, talked about his next book and a recent automobile accident. That same afternoon Otto Kahn dropped around before leaving for America. Then a Pasha talked about politics. Then a poet too drunk to keep off his knees.

The above is no intimation of a traffic jam on the stairs leading up to her studio. There were days, and even weeks, when she was undisturbed. What impressed me most was not the number of her visitors, but their attitude towards her. Men respond to women who are authentic.

Louise has just returned from America, after being away about a year. During that period she had absorbed enough contemporary Americana for a few more books. Being the sort of person who takes experience by the seat of the pants and doesn't let go, she plunged into every hectic milieu. She was pinched in speak-easies, held up twice, [made] a confidante of police squads, reported sick and reported dead. She was gassed with the bonus boys at Washington and her eyes still bother her.

The rumor that she was dead started an alarm in the Quarter. After it circulated about a month, I published it here as a report. At any rate, it was far too premature, and Louise is as active as ever.

I think she has always examined death. Her first play, *The Game*, written for the Provincetown Players when she was about 17, depicts life and death shooting craps for human bodies.[1]

In the dark days, when her husband, Jack Reed, was dying in Russia with a contagious disease, she rushed up to him, passed the horrified doctors, and embraced him. Her chance of survival, they told her a few minutes later, was one in ten.

A couple of years ago, she and her pilot crashed. The pilot died. "Your chances for survival," the doctors told her, "are one in ten." She's still here.

The fidelity exhausts her and eventually will destroy her. She welcomes every blister of experience, and Fate is only a snake. "I am so irregular myself," she says. "Sometimes I get up at 2 in the morning and walk along the Seine." Her nervous energy must be bottomless.

Last evening, we visited her historic boudoir, illuminated only by candles, four blocks from the Dôme. Everything one touches in Paris turns to history, and it may be declared that the room, over which Louise has reigned for eight or nine years, was the setting for a slaughter during the French Revolution. One abbot and 300 priests were killed in the garden.

On the floor and walls were odd treasures: ikons, Greek images, old manuscripts, Ming vases, totem poles and Turkish towels.

"This," said the female Epimetheus, pointing at small elephants in a row, "was a gift of Carl Van Vechten. Vincent Sheean gave me the devil-worship figures. D'Annunzio made this ring himself."

She wasn't boasting. She was only answering my questions.

Her arms and fingers glittered, and she looked like a staggering jewelry store.

"Where did you get all that?" I asked. She wore jade bracelets, blue sapphires, black pearls and moonstones casting moonlight.

She said the American Legion boys at Washington (which she had been covering for a syndicate) gave her the offerings.

Then I saw a lump of clay in progress. The piece, when finished, will be called *Male Conceit*.

So this poet and newspaper woman is a sculptor. Also composer, aviator, pianist, playwright, and the rest of the list. She gives Apollo a good workout.

Louise has already written two books on Russia. The third, contracted for by Harrison Smith, will be on Russia and her husband: *My Friend, John Reed*.[2]

When Jack Reed died in Russia, Louise changed. She lost a certain tangibility, and ever since she has lived as if every experience were her last. She is too thorough for revery, but will retain until the end, I think, enough chaos to make her interesting. Assorted visitors will enter her cloister on the Rue d'Assas, but perhaps she finds them, after John Reed, a bit absurd. She once wrote a poem beginning with:

> And there is a round absurdity
> Called the earth.[3]

Let's all be sentimental.

*
* *

1. Bald reports Louise Bryant's death in his column of 9 February 1932, (p. 96). See p. 23, n. 1.
2. See p. 23, n. 5. Bryant did not publish *My Friend, John Reed.*
3. Bryant apparently did not publish this poem.

Tuesday, 29 November 1932, p. 4.

Doris Carlyle, a woman who has always followed her urges, is back in Montparnasse. She is back with a black eye.

"I had a terrible time in Majorca," she told her friends at the Dôme. "Everyone tried to steal my money, and a fellow on the train bruised my sensitive skin." She rolled up her sleeves to prove it.

"Now I'm as broke as a scrambled egg," she shouted softly. "Can any of you pikers buy me a drink?"

They brought her more than one drink; they said they'd give anything for one more tale from the lips of this bursting Bohemian. Once she was the Queen of Greenwich Village. Then she graduated to Montparnasse, then to Majorca and back again to Montparnasse. It's the gypsy in her.

"In my Greenwich Village heyday I never was broke," Doris boasted. "When they gave the Pagan Route Ball, I was Astarte, crowned by the best writers in New York, and I did the Dance of Seven Veils."

"Once," she added, "I did the Dance of Eight Veils. After that night the Village broke up. I danced, I sang. I was an Epstein model. Once I drove a team of mules across the Andes."

"Gee!" everyone exclaimed.

"Montparnasse isn't big enough to hold me. Majorca is a flop. What can a poor girl do?" she wailed.

One night last winter she did something characteristic. To prove she was a real blonde, she proceeded to be a nudist—until a spry garçon stopped her. But she'll never lose her *esprit*. She'll always be a Bohemian. In the Quarter they call her "the girl with the orange beret."

Man Ray thinks New York would look much better if all the skyscrapers were laid on their sides. Don't ask him why. An artist never gives reasons.

Another idea of his is the virtue of gold.

"I'd like a golden automobile," he said, "a golden motorcycle or bicycle. Imagine Geneva on a gold foundation and golden bullets in time of war!"

Man Ray is a visionary, but all art is a wish. He says he likes the metal for its esthetic rather than its exchange value. It is a good light reflector, and it doesn't rust.

Imitation-gold background, says our Montparnasse modernist, is the latest thing in painting.

Last Friday we attended the vernissage of Man Ray's paintings chez Dacharry.

One of them, *Factory in the Forest*, was photographed by himself and is reproduced here. It has an interesting symbol; note the natural motive in the background, how it relieves the architectural motive in the foreground. Someone present suggested that the canvas nobly survived an attack of flies.

Gold-leaf or silver-leaf had been glossed over the surface of each canvas before paint was applied.

"I sought for a luminous background, and gold or silver leaf are good reflectors of light," said Man Ray. "Italian primitives used gold-leaf halos, a spotty arrangement which only resulted in large masses of paint. My interest in problems of light is the result of my experiments in photography."

Man Ray is really a photographer. Twelve years ago he gave up painting and arrived in Montparnasse to experiment with the camera. He still paints now and then.

"Photography," said Man Ray, "is the shorthand of painting. In another 50 or 100 years, the camera will entirely supplant the brush, and painters will have to get other jobs or become photographers."

Every argument I managed to interpose was overruled.

"The camera," said the photographer, "employs light and shade, *not the illusion of light and shade.* And the use of color will be accessible in our *métier.*"

He added that a good photograph misses none of the soul. "Even a snapshot can catch that," he said. I asked him to explain.

"I've come across snapshots in the Sunday editions of newspapers, and even weekday editions, which for emotion conveyed equal anything I've ever seen."

"Journalism is getting somewhere," I agreed.

"Photography," asserted its Messiah, "isn't much more than 50 years old, whereas art is 5,000. Give it a chance. It has taken us 500 years to see El Greco. The human eye must be trained to see a real photograph."

I saw several in his studio. He is giving a show at the Galerie Vignon, starting Friday.

"Has art no end?" I asked. "Yesterday it was painting, today artistic photography, tomorrow television. What will happen eventually?"

Man Ray frowned telescopically.

"Gold-leaf visions," he said, firmly. "Let's look forward to the Golden Age."

*
* *

Tuesday, 20 December 1932, p. 4.

*
* *

The expatriates' gift to literature is an anthology called *Americans Abroad.*[1]

I recommend this volume to the reader with the understanding that the reader is interested in faces. Forgetting the painful excellence of the contributions, you will find the book a screaming rogues' gallery of about half a hundred expatriates, each of whom sent his photograph along with his prose or verse.

What does W. C. Williams look like? Why does Gertrude Stein wear a hat like that? Does Henry Miller really resemble a saint? What's pleasant about Ezra Pound's death mask? Is Laurence Vail, standing on a mountain, about to yodel? Does Alfred Kreymborg look like Link Gillespie? What about Martha Foley?

It seems that everybody writing in Montparnasse has contributed words

123

and a photograph to this anthology. Their faces can tell you more than I can write.

Why an anthology?

It was Samuel Putnam's fault. The accompanying snap shows him sitting, like a hermit on a doorstep, in front of his chateau at Mirmande, wondering why he started it.

He didn't wonder long, because he placed the task on the grateful shoulders of Peter Neagoe who, even though he didn't originate the idea, deserves all the credit for its compilation. Neagoe is nearly as promising in the field of literature as his charming wife is in painting.[2]

The trouble with Putnam is that he does too many jobs in too short a time, and after getting out both volumes of *The European Caravan*, along with a few translations of Pirandello, and a few more that would fill a trunk, what does he do but knock out a novel.[3] Such energy frightens me. No wonder he decided to inter himself in Mirmande, where he soon found himself surrounded by appreciative friends, of whom Neagoe is only one.

"I am glad that my friend amply fulfilled his allotted task," Putnam said when last in Paris. "The *Americans Abroad* showed a great deal of industry on his part, and I am glad I didn't appoint someone else who might have bungled it." Neagoe is also the author of a book which has been banned![4]

But Putnam did get a shock when one of his publishers, Brewer, Warren & Putnam, suddenly flopped.[5] It was a trying interlude until he learned that the firm had sold out to Harcourt, Brace & Company, thus straightening everything out.

*
*   *

The heart of Bohemia is pinned on a small group seldom mentioned here. Of course they are French, but they come closest to the most convincing sighs of Murger.

I refer to that gay circle drawn around Fernande Barrey, known as an outstanding surromanticist—also known as the ex-wife of Foujita.

A couple of nights ago I was caught by that perpetual bubble and dragged up to her studio in the Rue Delambre. Kiki was there; so were Koyanagui and Mme. Petrides. There was a fellow called Paul Petrides—and there was Henri Broca, pale, delicate and convalescent. Broca, a brilliant caricaturist, cracked one night and was found wandering, weeping, about the streets through broken images. But he seems to have recovered.

Fernande laughed, sang and kicked her pajamaed legs at a Juan Gris.

"C'est la vie." A Victrola record laughed with her. Everyone danced in the dimmed blue lights, including the magpies and parakeets in cages. *"J'adore les Américains!"* shouted Fernande. *"Pourquoi?"* Fernande slapped her pajamas and screamed: *"Je ne sais pas!"* And everyone danced. And the evening wore on. And Fernande is reducing by taking plenty of exercise and eating seven onions a day.

She says Jun Foujita, now in Mexico, is coming back next month. Another gift of Santa Claus.

*
* *

1. See p. 63, n. 2.
2. Peter Neagoe's wife was Anna Frankeul. For an example of her painting, see Chil Aronson, *Artistes américains modernes de Paris* (Paris: Editions "Le Triangle," 1932), pp. 104-6.
3. *The European Caravan*, ed. Samuel Putnam, et al. (New York: Brewer, Warren & Putnam, 1931). Only one volume of *The European Caravan* was published. See p. 43, n. 1; p. 21, n. 8; p. 33, n. 1. Putnam published no novels.
4. The United States banned Neagoe's *Storm* in 1932. See p. 99, n. 3.
5. Brewer & Warren published Putnam's translation of Jean Cocteau's *Enfants terribles* (1930); Brewer, Warren & Putnam published *The European Caravan* (1931).

Tuesday, 10 January 1933, p. 4.

Bill Seabrook, a son of Montparnasse now living in Bandol, returned for a day. He stopped at the Hotel Lutetia long enough to visit the Dôme.

Bill is a great guy—all dolled up in a purple shirt and wine-colored tie to match. He looks rustic, savage and good-natured. He said: "In Bandol I live on the open plains. I have a big garden with turnips, rabbits and even turtles. My lop-eared hound thinks I'm God."

He's the author of *Jungle Ways* and other books on African voodoo, hoo-doo and doodoo. He believes in them.

His *Adventures in Arabia* and more recent *Air Adventure* will be run serially in French publications.[1]

"My book *Air Adventure* is a thrilling story of my flight to Timbuctoo," he said. "I had great difficulty writing it because of my eyes." Bill's eyes were affected by a recent automobile accident, but he says they see all right now. "I thought I was never going to finish that book, but somehow it got done."

The barman at the Lutetia brought us another cocktail.

Then I asked Bill what a slice of man tasted like. Once, at a savage ceremony in Africa, he had eaten a *filet d'homme*: a chunk of arm and a rump steak.

"It was very tough," he admitted, "and needed a lot of seasoning." Then he added, "But the savages aren't finicky."[2]

Bill said that Marjorie Worthington was keeping the home fires burning while he was away. Marjorie is writing another novel, *Ellen Abernathe*, all about a girl of 27 interested in sex.[3]

Aldous Huxley, one of the settlers in Bandol, expects to leave for America to see about his play which will be produced in New York. Huxley has just finished his labors on *The Letters of D. H. Lawrence*.[4]

And the Kislings are down there.

"Kisling almost caused a family riot," said Bill. "He wanted to paint a still life of Mediterranean fish, went to the market and bought about 60 pounds of the models.

"After about six days the models were guilty of an odor worse than a morgue, and his family and the neighbors ordered him to throw them out. But each day they looked more striking and the colors developed as rapidly as the odors. What is an artist to do? He went on painting. But I was too busy working to smell everything."

Such is life in a little city.

Julian Trevelyan, one of the younger artists, gave a party last week. About 35 painters (leaders in "aht") and about 35 writers (leaders in thought) were present.

The host wore the long, silk black dress of a Roman matron; he said it took him half an hour to get into it. He also wore fox furs and a wig of silver fuzz to make him look matronly.

The party was enlivened by miscellaneous noise, such as the banging of coffee pots and shouts of joy. (Hey! Hey!)

Someone said the host looked like George Sand, and all evening one of the poets wandered about on the verge of reciting his verse, but he couldn't find anyone to recite it to.

Everyone was wildly excited, and tea flowed like Swinburne's tears.

Julian is very Bohemian. Recently he hurried back to Montparnasse after spending some time in Mont Athos, a distant colony for men only.

"It is a wonderful place," said the artist. "No women are allowed in the colony. Even the animals are male and cows are nowhere to be found. Once a woman journalist tried to gain admission, disguising herself by padding herself like a man, but she was found out and ejected."

It seems that the monks liked Julian and regarded him with kindly curiosity, but one of them was a sadist and pulled the boy's long curly hair from time to time, nor would he desist until Julian, exasperated, threatened to slap him.

"Oh," the host sighed. "I must tell you about my swimming across the river that separates Albania from Serbia. The water looked so lovely and warm that I plunged in, knowing full well that a shark might catch me. In the 18th century they ate a deacon. Finally I reached the shores of Albania, stark naked and happy. It was a splendid experience!"

Julian is just wild about life and thought in the raw, and he says he wouldn't have missed the experience for anything. "We would stagger through the countryside and sing wild songs, startling the natives of the countrysides, and I took snapshots of the brigands as we sang ribald folksongs."

Oh, we were so thrilled by these tales.

Standing in one corner of the large, tastefully appointed studio, with his back to the fireplace, was the poet George Reavey, his face a bearded melancholy.

George was speaking quietly about the architectural symbolism of the age and of his next sequence of poems, *Nostradam*.

"It will be more formal than the Faust series," he remarked. "I favor the sonnet and the four-quatrain forms."[5]

A blue shaded light dripping from a covered lantern accentuated the pallor of his mood. But it obscured neither the flame of his widowed soul nor the glow of his metaphysical grief. For George is exalted by the nasty blows of introspection. There is a joy in weighing the universe.

"My poems speak of disaster and schism," George went on, and added a few remarks about the inviolability of his spiritual tangle.

The analogy between his poetry and his beard, he said, was that both had a natural growth. His beard, however, expresses what his poetry obscures.

A listener asked: "What is more unlovely than a woman?"
George didn't hesitate.
"A mushroom," he replied.

*

1. See p. 81, n. 3. William B. Seabrook, *Adventures in Arabia* (New York: Harcourt, Brace, 1927; London: Harrap, 1928); see p. 91, n. 2.
2. See p. 81, n. 4.
3. Marjorie Worthington wrote no novel entitled *Ellen Abernathe*. Bald refers to her *"Scarlet Josephine"* (New York: Knopf, 1933).
4. Aldous Huxley had no play produced in New York after *World of Light* (1931) until *Giaconda Smile* (1948). See p. 115, n. 3.
5. See p. 110, n. 1, n. 3.

Tuesday, 17 January 1933, p. 4.

*
* *

Was Helen of Troy a blonde? Was Xantippe really ugly? How tall was Josephine?

I asked Gwen Le Gallienne, but she didn't know. "Women," she said, "are so pathetic."

Languid and distant as ever, Gwen was reclining on a Louis XIV bench in Richard's studio. I was sitting on the window sill.

"What people ordinarily mean by beauty," said Gwen disdainfully, "is mere prettiness. We must mark a division between beauty and prettiness. The ordinary man is just taken in. What kind of beauty shall we talk about? Do you know anything about mid-Victorian beauty?—or Syrian or Chinese? Greek beauty is a dull myth." She waved a cigarette-holder, about a foot long, in the air.

"Women," she said, "are never real with men. Man is too much her livelihood, whether she be mistress, wife, or stenographer. They have to think: 'I mustn't expose my real self to a man.' "

"Who," I asked, "is the hardest boiled?"

Gwen blew smoke rings at one of her paintings on the wall. "The débutante," she said quickly. "The daughter of a rich father bleeds him to the nth degree. She sits on his lap and coo-coos him for another coat or necklace.

128

The father is the real sugar daddy, and she takes all she can get. Society girls try to act blasé because it's the fashion, I suppose. They try to act blasé before they know enough to come in out of the rain."

"College girls," Gwen went on, "give me a pain. A young thing at one of my teas—she wasn't more than seventeen—walked up to me and said, 'And what do you think of the League of Nations?' So intellectual, my God!"

Gwen is beyond cynicism. She has graduated to the stage of mute acceptance. We discussed the aristocracy of the soul. "It's the only aristocracy there's left," she said. I listened and wondered.

"Women must live on their senses all the time," she said in low tones. "They must do the giddy act: think of clothes, body and fitting emotions. This is a man's world, and men have everything in it. No wonder women must be shrewder than men to survive."

"What do you think of the Hollywood collection?" I ventured. "Do you think they're beautiful?"

For the first time in our midnight conversation, Gwen snorted.

"No! They are pretty, but not beautiful. We must make a distinction. Prettiness is dazzling, superficial, easy, sweet, perishable, evocative of nothing special. But beauty is more complicated. Ah! There you go into the deeper realms. What the world calls beauty is like the fashion. What I call beauty is a different thing."

"Take your cat," I said.

Gwen, stately but sensitive, sat up, her large, sobbing eyes taking [in] the cat.

"That explains my point."

"Explains what?"

"Look at my Siamese cat. Every clever woman, trying to imitate Garbo, is really imitating my cat. The feline animal is never really submerged, conquered. Women can't even approach an alley cat for grace, superb grace. A cat is perfection: tantalizing, maddening, independent. A clever woman tries to imitate it, but never gets there."

Gwen added that the closest thing to it was a simple farm girl, the kind generally pictured with the everlasting milk pail on her arm. "But even she is like a fresh cow, a Holstein. Farm girls turn so earthly afterwards. No imagination."

The seance was interrupted by a spontaneous charge of tears. I couldn't help it; I was drowning in chagrin.

"What are you crying about?" said Gwen, yawning in the palm of her left hand.

"It's your fault," I burst out. "It's your own fault. You killed half of my illusions about women."

She laughed with understanding. "Well," she said, "you have to learn some time. You're such a romantic kid."

I brushed away my tears. "Shake it up, will you Gwen?" I said. "You're going fine, and I'm half an hour late already. Shock me with further words." Then we talked about the laws of attraction.

"What is it?" I asked.

She didn't know, either. "What do you think?" she said.

I didn't know. "I don't know everything," I expostulated.

"I'm like Eva," she said. "My sister likes to look on, too."

"What's the most beautiful part of a woman?" I asked.

"You're talking to an artist now?"

"Yes."

"Well, first I'd remove the head; that's not interesting. Then I'd remove the legs. They're in the way. One goes in for choice fragments. Sculpturally, I am noncommittal."

*
* *

Tuesday, 24 January 1933, p. 4.

Listen to James Stephens:

"We are entering a New Era. Let everyone rejoice, for we have just begun to emerge from the darkness of the Jungle Generation. Our break with the past is the most complete in human history."

"What do you mean by the Jungle Generation?" I asked. Stephens has just returned from America.

"I mean the Jazz Age. We may call it Sex and Noise. The jazz epoch, with its destructive tendencies, is over; and a complete change is now in being. Discontent has become universal, but a New Content is being born."

Then I asked him if he saw any signs of the new energy in America.

"The Energy is there," he answered. "I saw signs of it in a few of the new poets, although I can't remember their names. But every artist may be full of courage; a New Synthesis is on the way."

We spoke of Joyce and Proust.

"They belong to the Jazz Age," said Stephens. "Their work is over, for they wrote prose epics that summed up social orders that have disappeared. Joyce and Proust belong to the dead Jazz Age. Even Paul Valéry has technique but no Content."

We spoke of George Moore who died last week.

"Moore dates with Flaubert and Zola."

I asked: "And now?"

"The slate is being wiped clean. The masters of this generation will be dead in ten years."

Stephens is a little man with a bald gloomy head. He has a mild rolling brogue, and as he spoke it appeared to me that in his mournful eyes there reposes the mirth of the ages. Stephens looks like a Buddha gone Irish.

"The Jazz Age," he said, "was a period of violence and destruction, of which the War was only a phase. The little movements in art—"isms," free verse—all died young. All that is forgotten. It was a woman's period. *Back of the whole Jazz Fact lies the woman.*"

My task here is to report Stephens' beliefs as significantly as possible. "The Jazz Age," he went on, "was violent and feminine—Sex and Noise. Look at the symptoms—Rodin in architecture. Even Nietzsche foresaw it.

"Woman has lost out. The Jazz Age has reduced her to a pleasure-giver and a parasite. Family ties have weakened and woman's domain has become deplorable. There may come into the male a distaste for the female through over-abundance of gratification." Which reduces sex to a cocktail.

"Can woman retrieve herself?" I inquired.

His eyes twinkled. "Maybe. If she decides to do all the labor in the New Era, man may appreciate her services again."

"Woman," he insisted, "is the pleasure-giver. Man is the pleasure-taker. For a man pleasure is restful and simple. For a woman it is hysterical and tainted with vanity."

We spoke of love.

"Love," he said, "is the domain of the male. Sex is the domain of the female. Only man can write a love story. After all, the realm of man is knowledge. A woman knows nothing beyond her greatest forte—self sacrifice." He added that the narrowing of intellectual attention must result in singular psychic storms. Also that man derives no lasting pleasure in being pursued by hideous females.

I said: "This New Era that you're talking about—can you mark it in any way?"

He said: "It will be linked with the scientific world. We will hear more about Einstein and Company, who must translate their mathematical formulae into appropriate words." He mentioned Bohr, Schrodinger, Eddington. "These men will open the oyster."

Stephens is writing a book of poems called *Absolute*. Something different from *The Crock of Gold* and *Deirdre*.[1] It will deal with a sphere that man can't deal with. But let us hope it opens the oyster.

*
* *

1. James Stephens apparently published no book entitled *Absolute*. Stephens, *The Crock of Gold* (London: Macmillan, 1912; Boston: Small, Maynard, 1912); *Deirdre* (London: Macmillan, 1923; New York: Macmillan, 1923).

Tuesday, 28 February 1933, p. 4.

*
* *

This brings us to the current number of *transition*, a magazine which for a few years has galloped in vain.

The present issue of the experimental magazine provides every indication that this one will be the last.[1]

In times like these, there is something clammy about challenges like "the crisis of language." The challenges were moderately stale even before the popular crisis.

I admire the editor, Eugene Jolas, artistically and personally; but his challenges are stale. I am afraid that Jolas seeks to convince by repetition.

But we are escaping from the modest purlieus of this strip. May it be added that vaudeville and soup grow cold, that "exuberance" should never develop into hysteria.

Blessed are the poets, and especially Richard Thoma. Every sonnet he composes is a favor to the eager world.

His recent epic is called *The Promised Land,* a place infected with whimsy.[2]

If at midnight you see a tall satanic man striding across the Carrefour, bare-headed and intense and burning, you will know it is Richard Thoma, the poet, collecting himself after composition and dreaming of future thought.

The theme of *The Promised Land* wrestles with the *Tree of Life,* on whose branches the hero discovers his heart, only to realize that the prize is an ordinary leaf.

There is something strangely dangerous, Machiavellian, about Thoma and his poetry. He writes subjectively about chaos, thus startling the reader. His last book was called *Green Chaos,* a title decided by his predilection for writing his verse in spinach-green ink.

Stuart Gilbert, in his enthusiastic introduction, reflects that the "so-called decadence brought forth a tragic splendor that the hygienic ecstasies of our enlightened age can never compass."[3]

The reader will not understand, and therefore not appreciate, the poet's references unless he takes the trouble to read the source books the poet has read. Thus, the term "Ygdrasil," meaning the tree of life, was borrowed from Scandinavian mythology. The spirit of Cocteau was not entirely absent.

Thoma is an able Montparnasse poet and will bear watching.

*
* *

1. *Transition,* 22 (February 1933). *Transition* continued until 1938.
2. See p. 115, n. 2.
3. Bald quotes, not entirely correctly, from Stuart Gilbert's foreword to Richard Thoma's *The Promised Land.*

Tuesday, 11 April 1933, p. 4.

The picture on this page shows Hilaire Hiler, George Antheil and myself. Hiler is the tall one, Antheil is in the center, and I was so self-conscious I forgot to light my cigarette.

We'll talk about Antheil first.

He has just come up from Cagnes-sur-Mer, easily punned, and expects to stay here. There is something musical about George, for at 26 he wrote an opera. His second, *Helen Retires*, written with John Erskine, will be run in America next winter.

Helen Retires is all about that old-fashioned blonde who literally went to hell to cheer up its guests.

Now he wants to make a sound film with Fernand Léger—something based on his ancient *Ballet Mécanique*, an *avant-garde* movie—in which the only actor is Kiki, who walks through it once without any clothes on.[1]

George says he hopes to be tranquil here, despite the fact that an Italian beauty, who accompanied him and his wife to Paris, is watching over him with considerable interest.

It was George who discovered Link Gillespie 12 years ago, when that overwhelming poet first landed in Paris.

"Link dropped [in] around 5 o'clock in the morning, just off the ship," said George. "He woke us up and said he wanted breakfast." Link then laid down his baggage: a suitcase containing an old shirt and a loaf of bread, a bundle of manuscript tied with a rope, and a mandolin. After George's wife prepared the breakfast, Link said he was on a special diet and couldn't eat it. So he broke off a chunk of his bread, reached in his vest for a piece of cheese, and ate.

Link is the author of "Amerikaka" and a long poem entitled "Orange Juice Sorry You Made Me Cry."[2] He hates the English language and invented one of his own, to the great delight of Gertrude Stein and *transition*. Someone once asked him to recite his poetry over the radio. He said he would. "Providing," he stipulated, "you set the microphone in a pig pen. Pigs eating must supply the incidental music." I don't know what became of that project.

There is a rumor that Link is running a speakeasy in Philadelphia. Customers pay one dollar and are required to bring their own liquor.

Hiler's party last Friday was a good rally.

People arrived from the four corners of Montparnasse, and a few dozen Right Bankers crashed the gate. John Mahon, an oilman, volunteered to serve the cocktails. John was kept so busy that after a couple of hours both his arms were tired.

Everybody was there, friends and enemies, but no one was hysterical. I saw John Cox, the mural expert; Lillian Fisk, poetic painter; B. Mathieu, of *The New Yorker* (B. arrived with her six manicured poodles, two of which wore red fezzes); Sam Weller, of the Black Guards, and author of *Necessary Luxuries*; Hilda Dashiell and her blue eyes.[3] One could get lost in them.

Lorraine Hamilcar was restrained from turning handsprings. Allen Ullman hovered over Margaret Lawrence, a belle from New York. A green-eyed redhead made a flying leap and landed on Sisley Huddleston's cheeks. Sisley, kissed like that, was so stunned he almost fell on Mary Widney.

In one corner, Leo Stein, author of the *A. B. C. of Aesthetics*, was sitting on the floor and lectured like Socrates before Nina and his other disciples. His next book will be called the *D. E. F. of Philosophy*.[4] Betty Boligard was being squired around a lot. But the hit of the evening was Jimmie Charters, who cleared the floor and did a Turkish dance. Hiler, the host, played the piano and sang Spanish jokes. Michonze, the famous Russian Surrealist, insisted on painting designs with a borrowed lipstick on a dowager's back. She became angry and there was quite a rumpus. But didn't I see them together a few minutes later, and didn't I hear her whisper to him: "Why do such things here?"

*
* *

1. *Helen Retires* was first performed in New York in February 1934. George Antheil and Fernand Léger did not make a sound movie based on *Ballet Mécanique*.
2. See p. 25, n. 1. Lincoln Gillespie apparently did not publish "Orange Juice Sorry You Made Me Cry."
3. Sam Weller did not publish *Necessary Luxuries*.
4. Leo Stein, *The A-B-C of Aesthetics* (New York: Boni & Liveright, 1927). He did not write *D. E. F. of Philosophy*. Nina Auzias was Stein's wife.

Tuesday, 9 May 1933, p. 4.

To the inexperienced eye Brancusi's recently finished black marble portrait of Mrs. Eugene Meyer might just as well be one of Mrs. Roosevelt or Clara Bow.

But the experienced eye, after studying the featureless block, will take Brancusi's word for it. Perhaps the best way to appreciate his conception is to walk very slowly several times around the black gleaming solid. Thus light falling on the object will fill your consciousness with a fusion of planes and an infinite number of profiles. The result is Mrs. Eugene Meyer, of Washington.

Brancusi's studio is in the Impasse Ronsin, just ten minutes from the Dôme, and I dropped over to see him last week. I don't go there very often because it's too far. Generally I prefer to meet the chosen artisans in the easy atmosphere of the Coupole bar. That's where you'll meet most of them, if you are interested. A good time to catch them is between 9 and 10 in the evening. As a rule they haven't a thing to say; but Brancusi interests me.

This accepted Roumanian sculptor is a little burly old man with a square-cut beard and broad shoulders; his eyes have the honest puzzling smile of a clean-living peasant. He works very hard: in addition to a slavish application to his noble calling, he makes his own furniture, develops his own photographic plates—he has even manufactured a home-made Victrola. Brancusi can tell you about Montparnasse 27 years ago when the Dôme was a coachman's restaurant, when the Boulevard Raspail hadn't yet been cut through, when the ambitious comers of that period —Apollinaire, Max Ernst, Paul Fort, the Douanier Rousseau—congregated in a squalid bistrot near the present Rotonde and dreamt of advancing art just another notch. And Brancusi is a bachelor, girls.

His portrait of Mrs. Meyer will be exhibited at the coming Tuileries show, opening next week.

A description of a sculptor's studio is just a waste of words. But you may be interested in one object I saw at Brancusi's. It's a vertical wooden form, spiral effect, mounting to the high ceiling. To be exact, the form is polyhedral rather than spiral; but the effect remains the same—spiral. Now!

"What's that?" I asked.

"All my work must evoke a sentiment. This line will be removed to the garden, where it will be elongated and elongated until it reaches about 600 meters in height. Then I want it placed in a public park so that man's eye may travel up along it until the eye sees infinity. It is a spear piercing eternity. It will release the imagination and lift man up, up, beyond the miseries of earth."

There's no harm in that.

*
*   *

Tuesday, 16 May 1933, p. 4.

*
*   *

Louise Bryant is popular; the flashing brunette gets all the men. They surround her like a wall, for Louise doesn't like to be alone. They follow her, they appear when she appears.

"I like to collect lonesome men," said Louise. "Some of these boys are unhappy or homesick and I talk to them and make them happy. Sure! Why not!"

For a while a rumor persisted that Louise was going to the homeland of a young Tahitian of royal family, whom she liked. "I changed my mind," said Louise yesterday. "It takes 23 days to get to Tahiti. That's too far, and it's a long way back."

Louise keeps late hours, and often is awake when Paris isn't. She goes and comes as she pleases. "Whose business is it?" she asks. Night before last a note was slipped under her door. The note was written on monogrammed blue paper.

> Dear Madam, I am indeed most sorry to trouble you, but thought you would prefer that I wrote to you personally than that I should complain to the Director of the Hotel.
>
> I and my friend who share the room next to yours find it *impossible to sleep* at night on account of the noises of moving about that come from your room, especially between midnight and the early hours of the morning. I think perhaps you do not realize that the ceilings and the walls of this hotel (like all the modern small hotels in France) are extremely thin, for *I am certain* you do not wish intentionally to disturb us.
>
> Please do not conclude that myself and the girl with me are "goody-goody" or women with narrow minds as we are *Quite The Contrary*, but we lead a healthy active life, and do like to sleep when we go to bed. *Will you consider us?*

Louise, curious, glanced through the keyhole and saw she was being watched. There was a moment of apprehension. Then she wrote a reply.

> My dear lady, I would be more than sorry to trouble anyone. And I

seldom offer advice to a person, but I am a Parisienne and if you came to Paris to *sleep*, I say it is quite the wrong place. If I heard a noise in the night and awoke and realized that people were happy somewhere I should be very pleased. If I did I should take a book and read, being a little sorry that I was not so happy myself, but I should never disturb their pleasure. If, however, you hear again any unpleasant sounds emanating from the privacy of my chamber I would not be too indignant if you would knock because perhaps I should not be aware of these noises myself and perhaps you could help me discover them.

My idea about the noises is that they emanate from the water pipes, which do not work very well on this floor. It would be extremely difficult for me to agitate the whole house by moving about. You make many mistakes in English. For example, Madam should always be spelt thus: Madame. Also you should say "my friend and I" and not "I and my friend."

Yesterday morning the two ladies called on Louise. "We only wanted to get acquainted," they said softly. They were tall, thin and hard; they wore neckties.

Louise ordered them out; then she roared.

*

Tuesday, 6 June 1933, p. 4.

George Antheil is sitting on the laps of the gods. His second opera, *Helen Retires*, has just been planted.

He showed me a cable from his collaborator, John Erskine, reading that the Juilliard Foundation will give the première next November or December, with the assurance of a good modern presentation. There is $40,000,000 back of that, and Erskine is president.[1] America is in the mood for new music.

Meanwhile George is having a difficult time in Montparnasse. He can't go anywhere, to be sure, without being approached by love-sick girls. Their constant closing in on him is like a sacred dance, of which only he could write the music. I feel so sorry for George. The girls pursue him shamelessly and clutchingly, each one protesting a heart broken into tiny little bits and offering him a piece without his asking for it. Is that love? To escape their soft growls of desire George often appears at the Dôme disguised in green glasses and a long white beard.

*
* *

Jimmie, colorful barman at Romano's, leaves next week for a summer's job in the new gay resort at Bandol. He'll be gone a month or two.

During his absence here, John Mahon may officiate. John is the snappy barman, oilman, man of the world, who helped open the College Inn with Jed Kiley about six years ago.

Jimmie says he is writing his Montparnasse memoirs now. The memoirs will probably be dedicated to Flossie Martin. Anyway, says Jimmie, she is responsible for the title, *This Must Be the Place.*

The story goes that some years ago two panicky Right Bank ladies had decided to go slumming in Montparnasse. They were searching for atmosphere, and weren't sure they were in Montparnasse.

At last they peeked dubiously in a local bar and were about to go away, when along came Flossie Martin crashing through the door and unleashing an unapproachable blast of one syllables. The ladies nudged each other. "This must be the place," they tittered and marched right in.[2]

Jimmie was so full of energy years ago he used to punch himself in the nose or cut his ears and let the blood flow to calm himself down.

*
* *

1. The Juilliard School of Music held the première of *Helen Retires* on 28 February 1934. John Erskine (president of Juilliard from 1929 to 1937) published his libretto as a long poem, *Helen Retires* (Indianapolis & New York: Bobbs-Merrill, 1934). In mentioning $40,000,000, Bald possibly alludes to Mary Louise Curtis Bok's subsidies to George Antheil, which finally totaled approximately $40,000. See Linda Whitesitt, *The Life and Music of George Antheil 1900–1959* (Ann Arbor: UMI Research, 1983), pp. 45, 52–53, 131–32, 243.

2. James Charters, *This Must Be the Place: Memoirs of Montparnasse,* ed. Morrill Cody, and with an introduction by Ernest Hemingway (London: Joseph, 1934). This edition has no dedication, but it includes the following on p. [5]:

> Walking ten feet or so ahead of me was Flossie, both of us on our way from the Dôme to the Dingo. As Flossie came abreast of the bar entrance, a handsome Rolls-Royce drove up to the kerb and from it stepped two lavishly dressed ladies.

For a moment they hesitated. They looked at the Dingo questioningly. They peered in the windows between the curtains.

Flossie, seeing them, looked her contempt. As she passed into the bar she tossed a single phrase over her shoulder: "You bitch!"

Whereupon the lady so addressed nudged her companion anxiously. "Come on, Helen," she said, *"This must be the place!"*

The American edition (New York: Furman, 1937) has a new subtitle, *Memoirs of Jimmie the Barman*, and the title-page reads, "as told to Morrill Cody." It is dedicated to Florence Gilliam. This edition is a heavily edited version of the 1934 text.

Tuesday, 25 July 1933, p. 4.

Let's say Montparnasse is a handkerchief.

You crumple it up and put it in your pocket. When you go away, you take it out and wave it at your friends. It makes a pretty spot of color on the thinning air. Montparnasse, with which I have been occupied too long, is not a sanitary bit of linen with which to wave farewell.

It is a filthy rag one drops into the nearest garbage can.

There was a time when it was a painter's rag. Then Cezanne and Modigliani and Zak and Picasso used it to wipe their brushes on. Even though a rag, it was clean enough at first. Cezanne wiped a blue brush on it. And Modigliani a green. Picasso preferred it for his rainbow brush, while Zak delicately tinged it with mysterious colors.

Was it a glad rag?

It was, and the flash of its tints enticed the world. In the whole world, people began to see the light. They wondered whence it came, they investigated, they were conquered. The spiritual gold rush was on.

But adepts are never so good as their masters, and those who followed in the tracks of Cezanne began to wipe *their* brushes on the same rag. Their colors weren't clean; the rag became dirtier and dirtier. But more and more adepts were drawn Montparnasse-wards. They were dilettantes, fakes. The true artists fled.

And then came the tourists.

Montparnasse became the supernal roost of the unclean and the wide-eyed. A few artists occasionally wandered in to sniff masochistically its degradation, and then they wandered out again. The rag was wearing out; not even a handkerchief lasts forever. Now that I am leaving it, that I am saying farewell to it, I insist that it has become so thin, so brittle, so precarious that one more good blow into it by an ambitious beetle—and *pouf!* It will fall into dust.

I've had a good time. I've seen them all: Derain and Braque and Chirico and Lillian Fisk and Foujita and Joe the barman. I've seen James Stephens and Huxley and Norman Douglas and Colette and Marie Laurencin and Brancusi and Paul Fort and—but this could go on and on; I no longer wish it to go on and on. I've seen the Coupole expand over the Quarter like a mushroom or like a weight-lifter's chest, the Select go Oscar Wilde and the Rotonde Nordic. I've seen the Dôme, that palace of cheap bliss, that ugly wart on the face of the earth, turn into an American Bar. I've seen all that— but it's all over now. I'm not deserting a sinking ship; it's been sunk for ages. You get something out of Montparnasse, and then it gets something out of you—just like bad liquor.

The writers—they took Montparnasse for a pen-wiper. Their ink is mixed with bile and venom, as only writers who cannot get into *Vanity Fair* know how to mix it. They don't use pens—they use machines, do they? Well, they took Montparnasse for a typewriter ribbon, and the frenetic smack of the keys against the roller gave them exercise, if little else.

Though not otherwise severing my connections with *The Tribune* I have decided to relinquish this column, and in so doing I am giving up my sympathetic ties with certain types and groups whom I've always admired. Farewell to my Montparnasse friends, who may be listed:

Modest intellectual artists.

Poets of the machine age, who ransack Sears Roebuck catalogues.

Poets of the night language, the chthonian plungers barking on the terrain of impressive obscurantism.

Sculptors, chiselers of time-space statues with concave breasts, and not only real hair, but dandruff.

Modern artists who do their tricks with wire and chewing gum, and don't call them Picasso.

Ex-Butter Merchants, gone literary, who compose esoteric dithyrambs on The New Economic Soul in between heavy meals.

Self-styled leaders of poets, who dispatch shrieking squibs from the sunken rim of the world to battle obscurity, who invent new spellings to remain afloat.

Benevolent old men who try to muscle in on literary circles by encouraging celebrities and by buying their work.

Literary females of yesterday, Montparnasse deserters, who choose to add decor to the Carrefour Saint-Germain with their arch and aging presences.

Disappointed wives who pretend they're masculine because it's smart and because they have given up all else.

Forty-year-old maids *just beginning to live,* who wear berets and are over-gay. Why can't a woman grow old like a man? Why must she battle every wrinkle of the way? I wish Samuel Johnson were here.

Nice people who drop into the Sphinx after dinner for dessert.

The trees in front of the Dôme, nourished by dead cigarette butts.

As I write this valediction I see the parade of silhouettes. What became of Flossie Martin, Harold Stearns, Homer Bevans, the Countess Eileen? What became of Samuel Putnam, who brought forth on this continent *The New Review,* conceived in liberty and dedicated to the proposition that almost anyone is literary? Where is Jolas now? Where is Link Gillespie, the unconquerable poet who fought so valiantly that words might escape their spelling? Whither hath fled flummery and mummery? Oh!

There were others: Gilbert White, the jocular nonpareil; Louise Bryant, who survives the rest; Harry McElhone, Scotch on the Right Bank and Bohemian on the Left; Ernest Hemingway, who is doing for a clumsy animal what Ziegfeld did for the American Girl; George Antheil, cherubic but gifted; Rona Benzie, who escaped to London; Michonze, the great Russian Surrealist, whose cartoons you have seen here now and then; Gwen Le Gallienne, with her Siamese cat and Blakean trance; Howell Cresswell, saintly, psychic, and simply a grand conversationalist; Erskine Gwynne, the boulevardier; June Mansfield, the girl with the golden face; Hilaire Hiler, a dean of American painters; Richard Thoma, the blossoming poet, whose capacity for black coffee has turned his orbit into green chaos; Marie Wassilieff, with her rag dolls and mysterious son.

They have had their period of ordination.

The eccentrics of Montparnasse? The poverty? The loose morals? The drunkenness? The anxious idealists? The crusaders? What a tradition! The only difference between a Left Bank bum and a Right Bank bum is a few francs. The Left Bank bums aren't trying to hide.

The world is leveled off. Montparnasse is Main Street, and the "plastic" moderns have won their battle against cliché. Even automobiles and furniture are going Picasso. The staunch army may disband. Gertrude Stein has crashed (of all things) *The Atlantic Monthly*, and her autobiography is accepted for publication by the Book-of-the-Month Club (meaning 90,000 copies virtually guaranteed). I'll bet anyone my new suit she cops the Pulitzer Prize.[1]

I think art should be put in its place; art is a solace, but no solution. Montparnasse might wait a while, because the world now is interesting. When the world ceases to be interesting, Montparnasse will have a nice new handkerchief, something to cover a new face. At present it covers a corpse. I am tired of jiggling a corpse.

*

1. Gertrude Stein's autobiography appears in the *Atlantic Monthly* (1933): "Autobiography of Alice B. Toklas. I," 151.5 (May), pp. 513–27; "When We Were Very Young: Autobiography of Alice B. Toklas. II," 151.6 (June), pp. 677–88; "The War and Gertrude Stein: Autobiography of Alice B. Toklas. III," 152.1 (July), pp. 56–69; "Ernest Hemingway and the Post-War Decade: The Autobiography of Alice B. Toklas. IV," 152.2 (August), pp. 197–208. *The Autobiography of Alice B. Toklas* (New York: Harcourt, Brace, 1933; London: Bodley Head, 1933) was not a Book-of-the-Month Club selection. Stein did not win the Pulitzer Prize.

Appendix

This appendix lists all of Bald's "La Vie de Bohème (As Lived on the Left Bank)" columns in the *Chicago Tribune* (European edition).

Tuesday, 4 November, p. 4.
Tuesday, 11 November, p. 4.
Sunday, 30 November, p. 5.
Tuesday, 2 December, p. 4.
Monday, 8 December, p. 4.
Tuesday, 16 December, p. 4.
Tuesday, 23 December, p. 4.
Tuesday, 30 December, p. 4.

1931

Tuesday, 6 January, p. 4.
Tuesday, 13 January, p. 4.
Tuesday, 20 January, p. 4.
Tuesday, 27 January, p. 4.
Tuesday, 3 February, p. 4.
Tuesday, 10 February, p. 4.
Tuesday, 17 February, p. 4.
Tuesday, 24 February, p. 4.
Tuesday, 3 March, p. 4.
Tuesday, 10 March, p. 4.
Tuesday, 17 March, p. 4.
Tuesday, 24 March, p. 4.
Tuesday, 31 March, p. 4.
Tuesday, 7 April, p. 4.
Tuesday, 14 April, p. 4.
Tuesday, 21 April, p. 4.
Tuesday, 28 April, p. 4.
Tuesday, 5 May, p. 4.
Tuesday, 12 May, p. 4. From Bouche-de-Loup.
Tuesday, 19 May, p. 4. From Mougins.
Tuesday, 26 May, p. 4. From Cagnes.
Tuesday, 2 June, p. 4. From Marseilles.
Tuesday, 9 June, p. 5.
Wednesday, 17 June, p. 5.
Tuesday, 23 June, p. 4.
Tuesday, 30 June, p. 5.
Tuesday, 7 July, p. 4.
Tuesday, 14 July, p. 4.

Tuesday, 21 July, p. 4.
Tuesday, 28 July, p. 4.
Tuesday, 4 August, p. 3.
Wednesday, 12 August, p. 4.
Wednesday, 19 August, p. 4.
Wednesday, 26 August, p. 5.
Wednesday, 2 September, p. 5.
Wednesday, 9 September, p. 5.
Wednesday, 16 September, p. 5.
Wednesday, 23 September, p. 4.
Wednesday, 30 September, p. 4.
Wednesday, 7 October, p. 4.
Wednesday, 14 October, p. 4.
Wednesday, 21 October, p. 4.
Tuesday, 27 October, p. 4.
Tuesday, 3 November, p. 4.
Tuesday, 10 November, p. 4.
Tuesday, 17 November, p. 4.
Tuesday, 24 November, p. 4.
Tuesday, 1 December, p. 4.
Tuesday, 8 December, p. 4.
Tuesday, 15 December, p. 4.
Tuesday, 22 December, p. 4.
Tuesday, 29 December, p. 4.

1932

Tuesday, 5 January, p. 4.
Tuesday, 12 January, p. 4.
Tuesday, 19 January, p. 4.
Tuesday, 26 January, p. 4.
Tuesday, 2 February, p. 4.
Tuesday, 9 February, p. 4.
Tuesday, 16 February, p. 4.
Tuesday, 23 February, p. 4.
Tuesday, 1 March, p. 4.
Tuesday, 8 March, p. 4.
Tuesday, 15 March, p. 4.
Tuesday, 22 March, p. 4.
Tuesday, 29 March, p. 4.

Tuesday, 5 April, p. 4.

Tuesday, 12 April, p. 4.

Tuesday, 19 April, p. 4.

Tuesday, 26 April, p. 4.

Tuesday, 3 May, p. 4.

Tuesday, 10 May, p. 4.

Tuesday, 17 May, p. 4.

Tuesday, 24 May, p. 4.

Tuesday, 31 May, p. 4.

Tuesday, 7 June, p. 4.

Tuesday, 14 June, p. 4.

Tuesday, 21 June, p. 4. From Juan-les-Pins.

Tuesday, 28 June, p. 4. From Juan-les-Pins.

Monday, 11 July, p. 4. From Juan-les-Pins.

Tuesday, 12 July, p. 4. From Cagnes-sur-Mer.

Tuesday, 19 July, p. 4.

Tuesday, 26 July, p. 4.

Tuesday, 2 August, p. 4.

Tuesday, 9 August, p. 4.

Tuesday, 16 August, p. 4.

[Thursday, 25 August, p. 4. Bald did not write this column. It is an unsigned article from the *Majorca Sun*.]

Tuesday, 30 August, p. 4.

Tuesday, 6 September, p. 4.

Tuesday, 13 September, p. 4.

Tuesday, 20 September, p. 4.

Tuesday, 27 September, p. 4.

Tuesday, 4 October, p. 4.

Tuesday, 11 October, p. 4.

Tuesday, 18 October, p. 4.

Tuesday, 25 October, p. 4.

Tuesday, 1 November, p. 4.

Tuesday, 8 November, p. 4.

Tuesday, 15 November, p. 4.

Tuesday, 22 November, p. 4.

Tuesday, 29 November, p. 4.

Tuesday, 6 December, p. 4.

Tuesday, 13 December, p. 4.

Tuesday, 20 December, p. 4.

Tuesday, 27 December, p. 4.

1933

Tuesday, 3 January, p. 4.

Tuesday, 10 January, p. 4.

Tuesday, 17 January, p. 4.

Tuesday, 24 January, p. 4.

Tuesday, 31 January, p. 4.

Tuesday, 7 February, p. 4.

Tuesday, 14 February, p. 4.

Tuesday, 21 February, p. 4.

Tuesday, 28 February, p. 4.

Tuesday, 7 March, p. 4.

Tuesday, 14 March, p. 4.

Tuesday, 21 March, p. 4.

Tuesday, 4 April, p. 4. Subtitle: "(As Lived in Chicago)."

Tuesday, 11 April, p. 4.

Tuesday, 18 April, p. 4.

Tuesday, 25 April, p. 4.

Tuesday, 2 May, p. 4.

Tuesday, 9 May, p. 4.

Tuesday, 16 May, p. 4.

Tuesday, 23 May, p. 4.

Tuesday, 30 May, p. 4.

Tuesday, 6 June, p. 4.

Tuesday, 13 June, p. 4.

Tuesday, 20 June, p. 4.

Tuesday, 27 June, p. 4.

Tuesday, 4 July, p. 4.

Tuesday, 11 July, p. 4.

Tuesday, 18 July, p. 4. Subtitle: "(As Lived in London)."

Tuesday, 25 July, p. 4.

[Tuesday, 8 August, p. 4. John Hastings wrote this column.]

INDEX

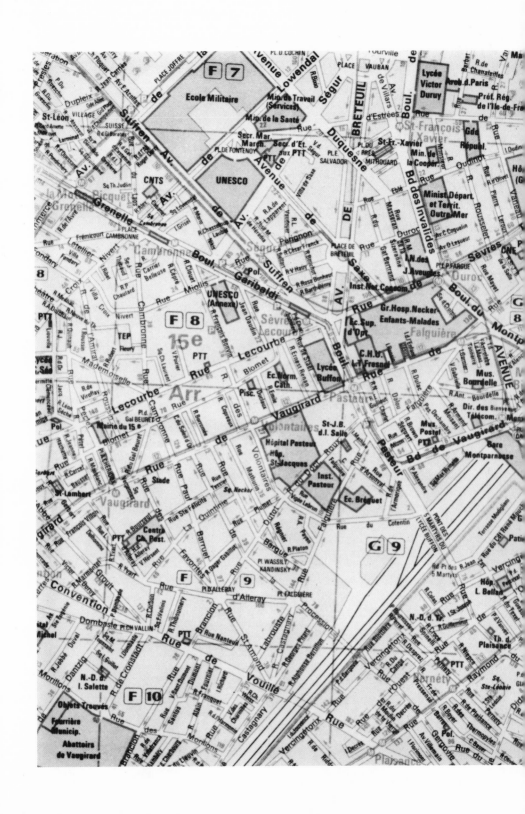